HOW TO READ A FINANCIAL REPORT

HOW TO READ A

WRINGING VITAL SIGNS OUT OF

Sixth Edition

WILEY

JOHN WILEY & SONS, INC.

FINANCIAL REPORT

THE NUMBERS

JOHN A. TRACY, Ph.D., CPA

Library of Congress Cataloging-in-Publication Data:

Tracy, John A.
    How to read a financial report : wringing vital signs out of the
numbers / John A. Tracy.—6th ed.
      p. cm.
    Includes index.
    ISBN 0-471-47867-9
    1. Financial statements. I. Title.
HF5681.B2T733
657'.3—dc21

PREFACE TO THE SIXTH EDITION

When I started this book we had no grandchildren; we now have 11 and one on the way. When the first edition was released in 1980 the Dow Jones Industrial Average hovered around 850. It reached an 11,700 high point in early 2000. You know what has happened to the Dow since then. As J. P. Morgan once said: "The market will fluctuate." Nevertheless millions of individuals have kept their money invested in the stock market, and stock investments are a large part of most retirement plans. Knowing how to read a financial report is as important as ever.

Stock values depend heavily on earnings and other information divulged in financial reports by businesses. Over the past few years many accounting fraud scandals have shaken investors' confidence in the reliability of financial report information. The large number of instances of financial reporting fraud—and the failure of the certified public accountant (CPA) auditors to discover these frauds—were a shock to me, and I think to most observers of financial reporting. The consequences of these accounting frauds pale in comparison with the consequences of the 9/11 terrorists attacks, of course. But the fallout from these financial frauds was widespread and caused billions of dollars of losses to investors.

Many asked what went wrong and how to fix things to prevent this sort of breakdown in our financial system from happening again. One result was the passage of the Sarbanes-Oxley Act of 2002. This piece of federal legislation made fundamental changes in how auditing and financial reporting will be done in the future. For one thing, a new Public Company Accounting Oversight Board having broad powers over auditing was established.

The demise of Arthur Andersen, one of the so-called Big Five CPA firms, caused by its conviction for obstruction of justice in the Enron case, was a wake-up call to the other four CPA firms—or was it? Only time will tell. Corporate executives and CPA auditors will have to operate under new rules in the future. Hopefully, these changes in the rules governing financial reporting and auditing will make the stock market a fairer place to invest money. We shall see.

All exhibits in this edition have been refreshed—to make them clearer and more contemporary. The exhibits were prepared from Excel work sheets. To request a copy of the work sheets please contact me at my e-mail address: tracyj@ colorado.edu. Now that I'm retired I have more time to read and answer my e-mails.

The basic design of the book remains unchanged. The framework of the book has proved very successful for more than 20 years. I'd be a fool to mess with this success formula. My mother did not raise a fool. Cash flow is underscored throughout the book. This cash flow emphasis is the hallmark of the book. It is the main characteristic that distinguishes this from other books on financial statement analysis. Of course I have made many updates dealing with the major developments since the fifth edition was released in 1999.

Not many books of this ilk make it to the sixth edition. It takes a good working partnership between the author and the publisher. I thank most sincerely the many persons at John Wiley & Sons who have worked with me on the book for more than two decades. The comments and suggestions on my first draft of the book by Joe Ross, then national training director of Merrill Lynch, were extraordinarily helpful. The continuing support of Debra Englander, executive editor at Wiley, is much appreciated.

I dedicate the book to Gordon B. Laing, my original editor. He laid a heavy hand on the book, which only now I see in fullest appreciation. His superb editing was a blessing that few authors enjoy. His guidance, encouragement, and enthusiasm made all the difference. Much to my sorrow Gordon died in January 2003. He was a true gentleman who taught me much about writing. His criticisms of my manuscript drafts were sharp but always kindly and supportive. Gordon took much pride in the success of the book—as well he should have! Gordon, my dear old friend, I couldn't have done it without you.

JOHN A. TRACY

Boulder, Colorado
January 2004

CONTENTS

1

STARTING WITH CASH FLOWS

Importance of Cash Flows:
Cash Flows Summary for a Business

Business managers, lenders, and investors, quite rightly, focus on *cash flows*. Cash inflows and outflows are the heartbeat of every business. So, we'll start with cash flows. For our example we'll use a company that has been operating many years. This established business makes a profit regularly and, equally important, it keeps in good financial condition. It has a good credit rating; banks are willing to lend money to the company on very competitive terms. If the business needed more money for expansion, new investors would be willing to supply fresh capital to the business. None of this comes easy! It takes good management to make profit, to raise capital, and to stay out of financial trouble.

Exhibit 1.1 on the next page presents a summary of the company's cash inflows and outflows for its most recent year. Two different groups of cash flows are shown. First are the cash flows of making profit—cash inflows from sales and cash outflows for expenses. Second are the other cash inflows and outflows of the business—raising capital, investing capital, and distributing profit to its owners.

I assume you're fairly familiar with the cash inflows and outflows listed in Exhibit 1.1—so, I'll be brief in describing each cash flow at this early point in the book:

- In the first group of cash flows, the business received money from selling products to its customers. It should be no surprise that this is the largest source of cash inflow, amounting to $51,680,000 during the year. Cash inflow from sales revenue is needed for paying expenses. The company paid $34,435,000 for manufacturing products that are sold to its customers; and, it had sizable cash outflows for operating expenses, interest on its debt (borrowed money), and income tax. The net result of these profit-making cash flows was a positive $3,430,000 for the year—which is an extremely important number that managers, lenders, and investors watch closely.

- In the second group of cash flows, notice first of all that during the year the company invested $3,950,000 in various assets. Where did this almost $4 million come from? The cash flow from its profit-making activities provided $3,430,000—or did it? Notice that the company distributed $750,000 of its profit for the year to its owners (stockholders), leaving only $2,680,000 for investing in its assets. So, the business borrowed more money during the year and its stockholders put a little more money into the business. Even so, the company's cash balance dropped $470,000 during the year—see Exhibit 1.1 again.

EXHIBIT 1.1—SUMMARY OF CASH FLOWS DURING YEAR
Dollar Amounts in Thousands

Profit-Making Cash Flows—Revenue Inflows and Expense Outflows

From customers for products sold to them, some from sales made last year	$ 51,680	
For buying and making products that were sold, or are still being held for future sale	(34,435)	
For many expenses of operating the business, such as wages and advertising	(11,955)	
For interest on short-term and long-term debt	(520)	
For income tax, some of which was due on last year's taxable income	(1,340)	
Net cash increase during year from profit-making activities		$ 3,430

Other Sources and Uses of Cash

For building improvements, new machinery, new equipment, purchase of goodwill, and the purchase of other assets that will be used several years	$ (3,950)	
From increasing amount borrowed on interest-bearing notes payable	625	
From issuing new capial stock (ownership) shares in the business	175	
For distributions to stockholders from profit earned during the year	(750)	
Net cash decrease during year from other activities		(3,900)
Decrease in cash during year		$ (470)

What Does the Cash Flows Summary NOT Tell You?

In Exhibit 1.1 we see that cash, the all-important lubricant of business activity, decreased $470,000 during the year. In other words, all cash outflows exceeded all cash inflows by this amount for the year. Without a doubt this cash decrease and the reasons for the decrease are very important information. The cash flows summary tells a very important part of the story of a business. But, cash flows do not tell the whole story. Business managers, investors in business, business lenders, and many others need to know two other essential things about a business that are *not* reported in its cash flows summary.

The two most important types of information that a summary of cash flows does not tell you are:

1. The *profit* earned (or loss suffered) by the business for the period.
2. The *financial condition* of the business at the end of the period.

Now, just a minute. Didn't we just see in Exhibit 1.1 that the net cash increase from sales revenue less expenses was $3,430,000 for the year? You may well ask: "Doesn't this cash increase equal the amount of profit earned for the year?" No, it doesn't. *The net cash flow from profit-making operations during the year does not equal profit for the year.* In fact, it's not unusual for these two numbers to be very different.

Profit is an *accounting-determined* number that requires much more than simply keeping track of cash flows. The differences between using a checkbook to measure profit and using accounting methods to measure profit are explained in the following section. Hardly ever are cash flows during a period the correct amounts for measuring a company's sales revenue and expenses for that period. Summing up, profit cannot be determined from cash flows.

Also, a summary of cash flows reveals virtually nothing about the *financial condition* of a business. Financial condition refers to the assets of the business matched against its liabilities at the end of the period. For example: How much cash does the company have in its checking account(s) at the end of the year? We can see that over the course of the year the business decreased its cash balance $470,000. But we can't tell from Exhibit 1.1 the company's ending cash balance. A cash flows summary does not report the amounts of assets and liabilities of the business at the end of the period.

Profit Cannot Be Measured by Cash Flows

The company in this example sells its products on *credit*. In other words, the business offers its customers a short period of time to pay for their purchases. Most of the company's sales are to other businesses, which demand credit. (In contrast, most retailers selling to individuals accept credit cards instead of extending credit to their customers.) In this example the company collected $51,680,000 from its customers during the year. However, some of this money was received from sales made in the *previous* year. And, some sales made on credit in the year just ended were not collected by the end of the year.

At year-end the company had *receivables* from sales made to its customers during the latter part of the year. These receivables will be collected early next year. Because some cash was collected from last year's sales and some cash was not collected from sales made in the year just ended, the total cash collected during the year does not equal the amount of sales revenue for the year.

Cash disbursements (payments) during the year are *not* the correct amounts for measuring expenses. Like sales revenue, the cash flow during the year is not the whole story. The company paid out $34,435,000 for purchasing and manufacturing costs during the year (see Exhibit 1.1). At year-end, however, many products were still on hand in *inventory*. These products had not yet been sold by year-end. Only the cost of products sold and delivered to customers during the year should be deducted as expense from sales revenue to measure profit. Don't you agree?

Furthermore, some of its product acquisition costs had not yet been paid by the end of the year. The company buys on credit the raw materials used in manufacturing its products and takes several weeks to pay its bills. The company has *liabilities* at year-end for recent raw material purchases and for other manufacturing costs as well.

There's more. Its cash payments during the year for operating expenses, as well as for interest and income tax expenses, are not the correct amounts to measure profit for the year. The company has liabilities at the end of the year for *unpaid expenses*. The cash outflow amounts shown in Exhibit 1.1 do not include these additional amounts of unpaid expenses at the end of the year.

In short, cash flows from sales revenue and for expenses are not the correct amounts for measuring profit for a period of time. Cash flows take place too late or too early for correctly measuring profit for a period. Correct timing is needed to record sales revenue and expenses in the right period.

The correct timing of recording sales revenue and expenses is called *accrual-basis accounting*. Accrual-basis accounting recognizes receivables from making sales on credit and recognizes liabilities for unpaid expenses in order to determine the correct profit measure for the period. Accrual-basis accounting also is necessary to determine the financial condition of a business—to record the assets and liabilities of the business.

Cash Flows Do Not Reveal Financial Condition

The cash flows summary for the year (Exhibit 1.1) does not reveal the financial condition of the company. Managers certainly need to know which assets the business owns and the amounts of each asset, including cash, receivables, inventory, and all other assets. Also, they need to know which liabilities the company owes and the amounts of each.

Business managers have the responsibility for keeping the company in a position to pay its liabilities when they come due to keep the business *solvent* (able to pay its liabilities on time). Furthermore, managers have to know whether assets are too large (or too small) relative to the sales volume of the business. Its lenders and investors want to know the same things about a business.

In brief, both the managers inside the business and lenders and investors outside the business need a summary of a company's financial condition (its assets and liabilities). Of course, they need a profit performance report as well, which summarizes the company's sales revenue and expenses and its profit for the year.

A cash flow summary is very useful. In fact, a different version of Exhibit 1.1 is one of the three primary financial statements reported by every business. But in no sense does the cash flows report take the place of the profit performance report and the financial condition report. The next chapter introduces these two financial statements, or "sheets," as some people call them.

A Final Note before Moving On: Over the past century an entire profession has developed based on the preparation and reporting of business financial statements—the accounting profession. In measuring their profit and in reporting their financial affairs, all businesses have to follow established rules and standards, which are called *generally accepted accounting principles* (GAAP). I'll say a lot more about GAAP and the accounting profession in later chapters.

2

INTRODUCING THE BALANCE SHEET AND INCOME STATEMENT

Reporting Financial Condition and Profit Performance

Business managers, lenders, and investors need to know the financial condition of a business. They need a report that summarizes its assets and liabilities, as well as the ownership interests in the excess of assets over liabilities. And, they need to know the profit performance of the business. They need a report that summarizes sales revenue and expenses for the most recent period and the resulting profit or loss. Chapter 1 explains that a summary of cash flows, though very useful in its own right, does not provide information about either the financial condition or the profit performance of a business.

Financial condition is communicated in an accounting report called the *balance sheet*, and profit performance is presented in an accounting report called the *income statement*. Alternative titles for the balance sheet include "statement of financial condition" or "statement of financial position." An income statement may be titled "statement of operations" or "earnings statement." We'll stick with the names balance sheet and income statement to be consistent throughout the book.

The term "financial statements," in the plural, generally refers to a complete set including a balance sheet, an income statement, and a statement of cash flows. Informally, financial statements are called just "financials." Financial statements are supplemented with footnotes and supporting schedules. The broader term "financial report" usually refers to all this, plus any addi-tional narrative and graphics that accompany the financial statements and their supplementary footnotes and schedules.

Exhibit 2.1 on page 9 presents the balance sheet for the company example introduced in Chapter 1, and Exhibit 2.2 on page 11 presents the income statement for its most recent year. Its formal cash flow statement for the year is discussed in Chapters 13 and 14; the summary of cash flows for the company presented in Chapter 1 has to be modified—as we'll see later.

The format and content of the two primary financial statements as shown in Exhibits 2.1 and 2.2 apply to manufacturers, wholesalers, and retailers—businesses that make or buy *products* that are sold to their customers. Although the financial statements of service businesses that don't sell products are somewhat different, Exhibits 2.1 and 2.2 illustrate the general framework of balance sheets and income statements for all businesses.

Side Note: The term "profit" is avoided in income statements. "Profit" comes across to many people as greedy or mercenary. Also, the term suggests an excess or a surplus over and above what's necessary. I should point out that you may hear business managers and others use the term "profit & loss" or "P&L statement" for the income statement. But this title hardly ever is used in external financial reports released outside a business.

EXHIBIT 2.1—BALANCE SHEET AT START AND END OF YEAR
Dollar Amounts in Thousands

	End of Year	Start of Year		End of Year	Start of Year
Current Assets			**Current Liabilities**		
Cash	$ 3,265	$ 3,735	Accounts Payable	$ 3,320	$ 2,675
Accounts Receivable	5,000	4,680	Accrued Expenses	1,515	1,035
Inventory	8,450	7,515	Income Tax Payable	165	82
Prepaid Expenses	960	685	Short-Term Notes Payable	3,125	3,000
Total Current Assets	$17,675	$16,615	Total Current Liabilities	$ 8,125	$ 6,792
Long-Term Operating Assets			Long-Term Notes Payable	$ 4,250	$ 3,750
Property, Plant, and Equipment	$16,500	$13,450			
Accumulated Depreciation	(4,250)	(3,465)	**Stockholders' Equity**		
Cost Less Depreciation	$12,250	$ 9,985	Capital Stock—800,400 shares at end and 770,400 shares at start of year	$ 8,125	$ 7,950
Goodwill	$ 7,850	$ 6,950	Retained Earnings	15,000	13,108
Accumulated Amortization	(2,275)	(1,950)	Total Owners' Equity	$23,125	$21,058
Cost Less Amortization	$ 5,575	$ 5,000			
Total Assets	$35,500	$31,600	**Total Liabilities and Stockholders' Equity**	$35,500	$31,600

Income Statement

The first question on everyone's mind usually is whether a business made a profit, and, if so, how much. So, we'll start with the income statement and then move on to the balance sheet. The income statement summarizes sales revenue and expenses for a period of time—one year in Exhibit 2.2. All the dollar amounts reported in this financial statement are cumulative totals for the whole period.

The top line is the total amount of proceeds or income from sales to customers, and is generally called *sales revenue*. The bottom line is called *net income* (also net earnings, but hardly ever profit or net profit). Net income is the final profit after all expenses are deducted from sales revenue. The business in this example earned $2,642,000 net income on its sales revenue of $52,000,000 for the year; only 5.1% of its sales revenue remained after paying all expenses.

The income statement is designed to be read in a step-down manner, like walking down stairs. Each step down is a deduction of one or more expenses. The first step deducts the cost of goods (products) sold from the sales revenue of goods sold, which gives *gross margin* (sometimes called gross profit—one of the few instances of using the term profit in income statements). This measure of profit is called "gross" because many other expenses are not yet deducted.

Next, operating expenses and depreciation and amortization expenses (unique kind of expenses) are deducted, giving *operating earnings* before interest and income tax expenses are deducted. Operating earnings is also called *earnings before interest and tax* (EBIT).

Next, interest expense on debt is deducted, which gives earnings before income tax. The last step is to deduct income tax expense, which gives net income, the bottom line in the income statement.

Side Note: Now and then, you may see references to earnings before interest, tax, depreciation, and amortization (EBITDA) expenses. You might ask why a measure of profit before deducting several expenses is calculated. The idea is to get a gauge on operating profit before the non-cash outlay expenses of depreciation and amortization are deducted, before interest expense is deducted that depends on how much debt is used, and before income tax that is contingent on how much profit is earned. Also, EBITDA is a rough measure of the cash flow thrown off from the operations of the business, before the cash outlays for interest and income tax are taken into account. EBITDA is not reported in the income statement.

Publicly owned business corporations report *earnings per share* (EPS)—which is net income divided by the number of stock shares. In the example, the company's EPS is $3.30 for the year. Privately owned businesses don't have to report EPS, but this figure may be useful to their stockholders.

In our income statement example you see six different expenses. You may find more expense lines in an income statement, but seldom more than 10 or so as a general rule (unless the business had a very unusual year). Companies selling products are required to report their cost of goods sold expense. Some companies do not report depreciation and amortization expenses on separate lines in their income statements.

Exhibit 2.2 includes just one operating expenses line. On the other hand, a business may report two or more operating expenses. Marketing expenses often are separated from general and administration expenses. The level of detail for expenses in income statements is flexible; financial reporting standards are somewhat loose on this point.

The sales revenue and expenses reported in income statements follow generally accepted conventions, which are briefly summarized here:

◆ **Sales Revenue**—the total amount received or to be received from the sales of products (and/or services) to customers during the period. Sales revenue is *net*, which means that discounts off list prices, prompt payment discounts, sales returns, and any other deductions from original sales prices are taken prior to arriving at the sales revenue amount for the period. Sales taxes are *not* included in sales revenue, nor are excise taxes that might apply. In short, sales revenue is the amount the business should receive to cover its expenses and to provide profit (bottom-line net income).

◆ **Cost of Goods Sold Expense**—the total cost of goods (products) sold to customers during the period. This is clear enough. What might not be so clear, however, concerns goods that were shoplifted or are otherwise missing, as well as write-downs due to damage and obsolescence. The cost of such inventory shrinkage may be included in cost of goods sold expense for the year (or, this cost may be put in operating expenses instead).

◆ **Operating Expenses**—broadly speaking, every expense other than cost of goods sold, interest, and income tax. This broad category is a catchall for every expense not reported separately. In our example, depreciation and amortization are broken out as separate expenses instead of being included with other operating expenses. Some companies report advertising and marketing costs separately from administrative and general costs, and some report research and development expenses separately. There are hundreds of specific operating expenses, some rather large and some very small. They range from salaries and wages of employees (large) to legal fees (hopefully small).

◆ **Depreciation Expense**—the portion of original costs of long-term assets such as buildings, machinery, equipment, tools, furniture, computers, and vehicles that is recorded to expense in one period. Depreciation is the "charge" for using these assets during the period. *None* of this expense amount is a cash outlay in the period recorded, which makes it a unique expense compared with other operating expenses.

EXHIBIT 2.2—INCOME STATEMENT FOR YEAR
Dollar Amounts in Thousands, Except Earnings per Share

Sales Revenue	$52,000
Cost of Goods Sold Expense	33,800
Gross Margin	$18,200
Operating Expenses	12,480
Depreciation Expense	785
Amortization Expense	325
Operating Earnings	$ 4,610
Interest Expense	545
Earnings before Income Tax	$ 4,065
Income Tax Expense	1,423
Net Income	$ 2,642
Earnings per Share	$3.30

• ***Amortization Expense***—the portion of the purchase costs of the *intangible* assets of the business that is recorded to expense in one period. In this example the business has only one type of such assets-*goodwill*. Amortization expense is recorded each period to recognize the gradual using up or expiration of the usefulness and value of its goodwill assets. Like depreciation, this expense does not require a cash outlay in the period that it is recorded as an expense; it is in the nature of a write-down of an asset.

• ***Interest Expense***—the amount of interest on debt (interest-bearing liabilities) for the period. Other types of financing charges may also be included, such as loan origination fees.

• ***Income Tax Expense***—the total amount due the government (both federal and state) on the amount of taxable income of the business during the period. Taxable income is multiplied by the appropriate tax rates. The income tax expense does *not* include other types of taxes, such as unemployment and Social Security taxes on the company's payroll. These other, non-income taxes are included in operating expenses.

Balance Sheet

The balance sheet shown in Exhibit 2.1 on page 9 follows the standardized format regarding the classification and ordering of assets, liabilities, and ownership interests in the business. Financial institutions, public utilities, railroads, and some other specialized businesses use different balance sheet layouts. However, manufacturers and retailers, as well as the large majority of other types of businesses follow the basic format presented in Exhibit 2.1.

On the left side the balance sheet lists *assets*. On the right side the balance sheet lists the *liabilities* of the business, which have a first claim on the assets. The sources of ownership (equity) capital in the business are presented below the liabilities, to emphasize that the liabilities have the higher or prior claim on the assets. The owners, or equity holders in a business (the stockholders of a business corporation) have a secondary claim on the assets—after its liabilities are satisfied.

Each separate asset, liability, and owners' equity reported in a balance sheet is called an *account*. Every account has a name (title) and a dollar amount, which is called its balance. For instance, from Exhibit 2.1:

Name of Account	*Amount (Balance) of Account*
Inventory	$8,450,000

The other dollar amounts in the balance sheet are either subtotals or totals of account balances. For example, the amount for "Total Current Assets" does not represent an account but rather the subtotal of the four accounts making up this group of accounts. A line is drawn above a subtotal or total, indicating account balances are being added. A double underline (such as for "Total Assets") indicates the last amount in a column. Notice also the double underline below "Net Income" in the income statement (Exhibit 2.2), indicating it's the last number in the column. (In contrast, putting a double underline below the "Earnings per Share" figure in the income statement is a matter of taste or personal preference.)

The balance sheet is prepared at the close of business on the last day of the income statement period. For example, if the income statement is for the year ending June 30, 2004, the balance sheet is prepared at midnight June 30, 2004. The amounts reported in the balance sheet are the balances of the accounts at that precise moment in time. The financial condition of the business is frozen for one split second.

You should keep in mind that the balance sheet does not report the total flows into and out of the assets, liabilities, and owners' equity accounts during a period. Only the ending balances at the moment the balance sheet is prepared are reported for the accounts. For example, the company reports an ending cash balance of $3,265,000 (see Exhibit 2.1). Can you tell the total cash inflows and outflows for the year? No, not from the balance sheet.

By the way, even business reporters occasionally seem a little confused on this point. Consider the following quote from a recent article about a company: "It has a strong balance sheet, with $5.6 billion in revenue ..." (the *Wall Street Journal*, May 18,

1998, page B1). Revenue is reported in the income statement, not the balance sheet!

The accounts reported in the balance sheet are not thrown together haphazardly in no particular order. Balance sheet accounts are subdivided into the following classes, or basic groups, in the following order of presentation:

Left Side	Right Side
Current assets	Current liabilities
Long-term operating assets	Long-term liabilities
Other assets	Owners' equity

Current assets are cash and other assets that will be converted into cash during one *operating cycle*. The operating cycle refers to the sequence of buying or manufacturing products, holding the products until sale, selling the products, waiting to collect the receivables from the sales, and finally receiving cash from customers. This sequence is the most basic rhythm of a company's operations; it's repeated over and over. The operating cycle may be short, only 60 days or less, or it may be relatively long, perhaps 180 days or more.

Assets not directly required in the operating cycle, such as marketable securities held as temporary investments or short-term loans made to employees, are included in the current asset class if they will be converted into cash during the coming year. A business pays in advance for some costs of operations that will not be charged to expense until next period. These *prepaid expenses* are included in current assets, as you see in Exhibit 2.1.

The second group of assets is labeled "Long-Term Operating Assets" in the balance sheet. These assets are not held for sale to customers; rather they are used in the operations of the business. Broadly speaking, these assets fall into two groups: *tangible* and *intangible* assets. Tangible assets have physical existence, such as machines and buildings. Intangible assets do not have physical existence but they have legally protected rights such as patents or give a business an important competitive advantage such as goodwill.

The tangible assets of the business are reported in the "Property, Plant, and Equipment" account—see Exhibit 2.1 again. These are also called *fixed assets*, although this term is generally not used in formal balance sheets. The word "fixed" is a little strong; these assets are not really fixed or permanent, except for the land owned by a business. More accurately, these assets are the long-term operating resources used over several years—such as buildings, machinery, equipment, trucks, forklifts, furniture, computers, telephones, and so on.

The cost of fixed assets—with the exception of land—is gradually charged off over their useful lives. Each period of use thereby bears its share of the total cost of each fixed asset. This apportionment of the cost of fixed assets over their useful lives is called *depreciation*. The amount of depreciation for one year is reported as an expense in the income statement (see Exhibit 2.2, page 11). The cumulative amount that has been recorded as depreciation expense since the date of acquisition is reported in the *accumulated depreciation* account in the balance sheet (see Exhibit 2.1, page 9). The balance in the accumulated depreciation account is deducted from the original cost of the fixed assets.

In the example, the company has only one type of intangible long-term operating asset—*goodwill*. The purchase costs of the various elements that make up this key asset are allocated over the predicted useful lives of each component, like the costs of the company's various fixed assets are allocated over their predicted useful lives. The amount allocated to each period is called *amortization expense*. The cumulative amount or recorded amortization expense since the dates of acquisition is reported in the *accumulated amortization* account (see Exhibit 2.1, page 9). The balance in this account is deducted from the cost of goodwill. (In their balance sheets some businesses report only the net amount of un-amortized cost.)

Other assets is a catchall title for those assets that don't fit in current assets or in the long-term operating asset classes. The company in this example does not have any such "other" assets.

The official definition of *current liabilities* runs 200 words, plus a long footnote to boot. So, I have to be brief here. The accounts reported in the current liabilities class are short-term liabilities that for the most part depend on the conversion of current assets into cash for their payment. Also, other debts (borrowed money) that will come due within one year from the balance sheet date are put in this group. In our example, there are four accounts in current liabilities (please see Exhibit 2.1, page 9 again).

Long-term liabilities are those whose maturity dates are more than one year after the balance sheet date. There's only one such account in our example. Either in the balance sheet or in a footnote, the maturity dates, interest rates, and other relevant provisions of all long-term liabilities are disclosed. To simplify, no footnotes are included with the balance sheet (Chapter 16 discusses footnotes).

Liabilities are claims on the assets of a business; cash or other assets that will be later converted into cash will be used to pay the liabilities. (Also, assets generated by future profit earned by the business will be available to pay its liabilities.) Clearly, all liabilities of a business must be reported in its balance sheet to give a complete picture of the financial condition of a business.

Liabilities are also sources of assets. For example, cash increases when a business borrows money, of course. Inventory increases when a business buys products on credit and incurs a liability that will be paid later. Also, a business usually has liabilities for unpaid expenses. The company has not yet used cash to pay these liabilities.

I mention this to point out another reason for reporting liabilities in the balance sheet, and that is to account for the sources of the company's assets—to answer the question: Where did the company's total assets come from? A complete picture of the financial condition of a business should show where the company's assets came from.

Some of the total assets of a business come not from liabilities but from its owners. The owners invest money in the business and they allow the business to retain some of its profit, which is not distributed to them. The *stockholders' equity* accounts in the balance sheet reveal where the rest of the company's total assets came from. Notice in Exhibit 2.1 there are two stockholders' (owners') equity sources—*capital stock* and *retained earnings*.

When owners (stockholders of a business corporation) invest capital in the business, the capital stock account is increased.* Net income earned by a business less the amount distributed to owners increases the retained earnings account. The nature of retained earnings can be confusing and, therefore, I explain this account in more depth at the appropriate places in the book. Just a quick word of advice here: Retained earnings is *not*—I repeat, is *not*—an asset.

*Many business corporations issue *par value* stock shares. The shares have to be issued for a certain minimum amount, called the par value. The corporation may issue the shares for more than par value. The excess over par value is put in a second account called "Paid-in Capital in Excess of Par Value." This is not shown in the balance sheet example, as the separation between the two accounts has little practical significance.

3

PROFIT ISN'T EVERYTHING

The Threefold Task of Managers:
Profit, Financial Condition, and Cash Flow

The income statement reports the profit performance of a business. The ability of managers to make sales and to control expenses, and thereby to earn profit, is summarized in the income statement. Earning adequate profit is the key for survival and the business manager's most important financial imperative. But the bottom line is not the end of the manager's job, not by a long shot!

To earn profit and stay out of trouble, managers must control the *financial condition* of the business. This means, among other things, keeping assets and liabilities within proper limits and proportions relative to each other and relative to the sales revenue and expenses of the business. Managers must, in particular, prevent cash shortages that would cause the business to default on its liabilities when they come due, or not be able to meet its payroll on time.

Business managers really have a threefold task: earning enough profit, controlling the company's assets and liabilities, and preventing cash-outs. Earning profit by itself does not guarantee survival and good cash flow. A business manager cannot manage profit without also managing the changes in financial condition caused by sales and expenses that produce profit. Making profit may actually cause a temporary drain on cash rather than provide cash.

A business manager should use his or her income statement to evaluate profit performance and to ask a whole raft of profit-oriented questions. Did sales revenue meet the goals and objectives for the period? Why did sales revenue increase compared with last period? Which expenses increased more or less than they should have? And many more such questions. These profit analysis questions are absolutely essential. But the manager can't stop at the end of these questions.

Beyond profit analysis, business managers should move on to financial condition analysis and cash flow analysis. In large business corporations the responsibility for financial condition and cash flow usually is separated from profit responsibility. The chief financial officer (CFO) is responsible for financial condition and cash flow; managers of other organization units are responsible for sales and expenses. In large corporations the chief executive and board of directors oversee the policies of the CFO. They need to see the big picture, which includes all three financial aspects of the business—profit, financial condition, and cash flow.

In smaller businesses, however, the president or the owner/manager is directly and totally involved in financial condition and cash flow. There's no one to delegate these responsibilities to.

The Trouble with Conventional Financial Statement Reporting

Unfortunately, the way financial statements are presented to business managers and other interested readers does not pave the way for understanding how making profit drives the financial condition and cash flow of the business. You can miss the vital interplay between the income statement and the balance sheet because each statement is presented like a tub standing on its own feet; interconnections between these two financial statements are not made explicit.

Exhibits 2.1 and 2.2 in Chapter 2 present the balance sheet and income statement for a business, as you would see these two primary financial statements. Each of the two statements stands alone, by itself, which is the standard way of presenting financial statements in a financial report. There is no clear trail of the crossover effects between these two basic financial statements. The statements are presented on the assumption that readers understand the couplings and linkages between the two statements and that readers make appropriate comparisons.

In addition to the balance sheet and income statement, a third basic financial statement is required to be included in external financial reports that are released outside the business—the *statement of cash flows*. Business managers, as well as creditors and investors, need a cash flow statement that summarizes the major sources and uses of cash during the period. So, you may well ask: Where is the cash flow statement?

Chapter 1 presents a cash flows summary of the business for the year (Exhibit 1.1, page 3). Of course it's a correct summary, but it's not in the recommended format for external financial reporting to the owners and creditors of a business. Financial reporting standards demand a different format, which I explain in Chapters 13 and 14. At this point we'll stick with the cash flows summary introduced in Chapter 1; its layout is much easier to understand.

The main message of this chapter is that the three basic financial statements fit together like tongue-in-groove woodwork. The income statement, balance sheet, and cash flows statement (summary) interlock with one another, which the following discussion illustrates.

The Interlocking Nature
of Financial Statements

The following three exhibits demonstrate how the financial statements of a business are interconnected. Exhibit 3.1 shows the lines of connection between the income statement and the balance sheet. Notice in passing that the balance sheet is presented in a vertical format, called the "report form"—assets on top, and liabilities and stockholders' equity below. In fact, many balance sheets are presented in the report form.

Sales revenue drives the *accounts receivable* asset account—see the first line of connection in Exhibit 3.1. Cost of goods sold expense drives the *inventory* asset account. See the second line of connection in the exhibit. And so on. We'll move carefully through each of these connections one at a time in the following chapters. Chapter 4 explores the linkage between sales revenue in the income statement and accounts receivable in the balance sheet. Then each connection is explored in successive chapters.

Notice in Exhibit 3.1 that accounts payable and accrued expenses are each divided into two parts, or subaccounts. There are two separate sources for each of these liabilities, which are discussed separately in later chapters. Typically businesses report only one amount for accounts payable and one amount for accrued expenses. However, a business may provide more detail for each of these basic types of liabilities. Financial reporting practices differ somewhat in this area.

Exhibit 3.1 presents the balance sheet of the business at the end of the year, at midnight on the last day of the year for which the income statement is prepared. Now think back to the start of the year if you would—see Exhibits 2.1 and 3.2. Virtually all the company's assets, liabilities, and owners' equity sources had different balances at the *start* of the year. Certain of these changes have the effect of increasing or decreasing the amount of cash flow from the company's profit-making activities for the year.

In other words, the net cash increase (or decrease) during the year from its revenue and expenses depends on the changes in certain of the company's assets and liabilities. Exhibit 3.2 shows these connections. Notice that the lines of connection go from the changes in the balance sheet to the cash flows from sales revenue and for expenses.

The direction of the lines means that the changes in the assets and liabilities directly affect the cash flow from sales revenue and for expenses. The end result is that the cash increase from the company's profit-making activities for the year is $3,430,000, which compared with its $2,642,000 net income is a fairly significant difference. In the example, for the year the company's cash flow from profit is $788,000 higher than its profit for the year. In other situations cash flow from profit could be much less than net income.

EXHIBIT 3.1—CONNECTIONS BETWEEN INCOME STATEMENT AND BALANCE SHEET
Dollar Amounts in Thousands

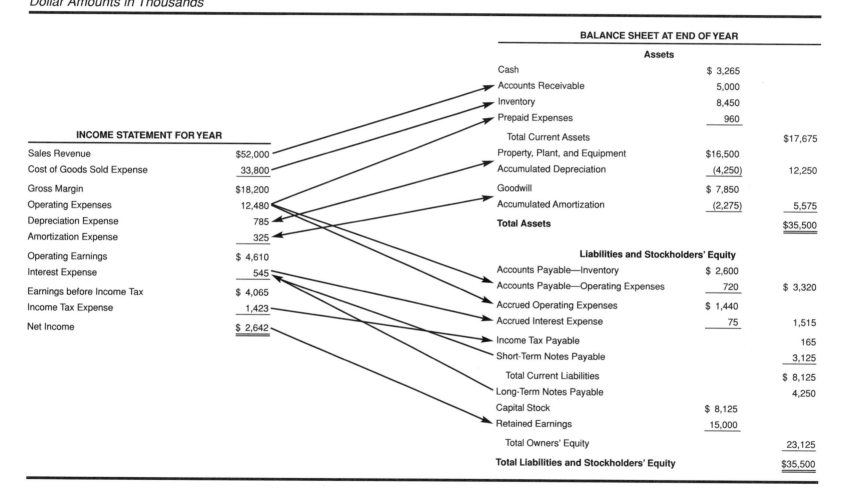

BALANCE SHEET AT END OF YEAR

Assets

Cash	$ 3,265	
Accounts Receivable	5,000	
Inventory	8,450	
Prepaid Expenses	960	
Total Current Assets		$17,675
Property, Plant, and Equipment	$16,500	
Accumulated Depreciation	(4,250)	12,250
Goodwill	$ 7,850	
Accumulated Amortization	(2,275)	5,575
Total Assets		$35,500

Liabilities and Stockholders' Equity

Accounts Payable—Inventory	$ 2,600	
Accounts Payable—Operating Expenses	720	$ 3,320
Accrued Operating Expenses	$ 1,440	
Accrued Interest Expense	75	1,515
Income Tax Payable		165
Short-Term Notes Payable		3,125
Total Current Liabilities		$ 8,125
Long-Term Notes Payable		4,250
Capital Stock	$ 8,125	
Retained Earnings	15,000	
Total Owners' Equity		23,125
Total Liabilities and Stockholders' Equity		$35,500

INCOME STATEMENT FOR YEAR

Sales Revenue	$52,000
Cost of Goods Sold Expense	33,800
Gross Margin	$18,200
Operating Expenses	12,480
Depreciation Expense	785
Amortization Expense	325
Operating Earnings	$ 4,610
Interest Expense	545
Earnings before Income Tax	$ 4,065
Income Tax Expense	1,423
Net Income	$ 2,642

EXHIBIT 3.2—CONNECTIONS BETWEEN BALANCE SHEET CHANGES AND CASH FLOWS FROM PROFIT-MAKING ACTIVITIES FOR YEAR

Dollar Amounts in Thousands

BALANCE SHEET at	End of Year	Start of Year	Change	PROFIT-MAKING ACTIVITIES FOR YEAR	Income Statement	Cash Flows
Cash	$ 3,265	$ 3,735	$ (470)	Sales	$ 52,000	
Accounts Receivable	5,000	4,680	320	Deduct $320 Increase		$51,680
Inventory	8,450	7,515	935	Cost of Products	(33,800)	
Prepaid Expenses	960	685	275	Add $935 Increase		
Property, Plant, and Equipment	16,500	13,450	3,050	Deduct $300 Increase		(34,435)
Accumulated Depreciation	(4,250)	(3,465)	(785)	Operating Expenses	(12,480)	
Goodwill	7,850	6,950	900	Add $275 Increase		
Accumulated Amortization	(2,275)	(1,950)	(325)	Deduct $345 Increase		
Total Assets	**$35,500**	**$31,600**		Deduct $455 Increase		(11,955)
				Depreciation Expense	(785)	0
Accounts Payable—Inventory	$ 2,600	$ 2,300	$ 300	Amortization Expense	(325)	0
Accounts Payable—Operating Expenses	720	375	345	Interest on Debt	(545)	
Accrued Operating Expenses	1,440	985	455	Deduct $25 Increase		(520)
Accrued Interest Expense	75	50	25	Income Tax	(1,423)	
Income Tax Payable	165	82	83	Deduct $83 Increase		(1,340)
Short-Term Notes Payable	3,125	3,000	125			
Long-Term Notes Payable	4,250	3,750	500	**Bottom-Line Profit, or Net Income**	**$ 2,642**	
Capital Stock	8,125	7,950	175	**Cash Increase from Profit-Making Activities**		**$ 3,430**
Retained Earnings	15,000	13,108	1,892			
Total Liabilities and Stockholders' Equity	**$35,500**	**$31,600**				

EXHIBIT 3.3—CONNECTIONS BETWEEN BALANCE SHEET CHANGES AND OTHER, NONPROFIT SOURCES AND USES OF CASH FOR YEAR

Dollar Amounts in Thousands

BALANCE SHEET at	End of Year	Start of Year	Change
Cash	$ 3,265	$ 3,735	$ (470)
Accounts Receivable	5,000	4,680	320
Inventory	8,450	7,515	935
Prepaid Expenses	960	685	275
Property, Plant, and Equipment	16,500	13,450	3,050
Accumulated Depreciation	(4,250)	(3,465)	(785)
Goodwill	7,850	6,950	900
Accumulated Amortization	(2,275)	(1,950)	(325)
Total Assets	**$35,500**	**$31,600**	
Accounts Payable—Inventory	$ 2,600	$ 2,300	$ 300
Accounts Payable—Operating Expenses	720	375	345
Accrued Operating Expenses	1,440	985	455
Accrued Interest Expense	75	50	25
Income Tax Payable	165	82	83
Short-Term Notes Payable	3,125	3,000	125
Long-Term Notes Payable	4,250	3,750	500
Capital Stock	8,125	7,950	175
Retained Earnings	15,000	13,108	1,892
Total Liabilities and Stockholders' Equity	**$35,500**	**$31,600**	

NONPROFIT CASH FLOWS FOR YEAR

Purchasing Long-Term Operating Assets		
Property, Plant, and Equipment	$(3,050)	
Goodwill	(900)	$(3,950)
Increasing Debt		
Short-Term Notes Payable	$ 125	
Long-Term Notes Payable	500	625
Issuing Additional Capital Stock Shares		175
Paying Dividends to Shareholders		(750)
Net Cash Decrease from Other Sources and Uses		$(3,900)
Cash Increase from Profit-Making Activities—Exhibit 3.2		3,430
Decrease in Cash during Year		$ (470)

During the year the business had other, nonprofit cash flows that changed certain assets, liabilities, and owners' equities. These are shown in Exhibit 3.3. Notice that the lines of connection go from the cash flow sources and uses to their corresponding balance sheet accounts. The cash flow sources and uses drive the changes in the balance sheet. In contrast, the balance sheet changes shown in Exhibit 3.2 drive the cash flows from profit-making activities.

You really can't swallow all the information in Exhibits 3.1, 3.2, and 3.3 in one gulp. You have to drink one sip at a time. The three exhibits provide road maps that we'll refer to frequently in the following chapters—so that we don't lose sight of the big picture as we travel down the particular highways of connection between the financial statements.

Before moving on, let me stress that financial statements are not presented with lines of connection as shown in Exhibits 3.1, 3.2, and 3.3. Accountants assume that the financial statement readers mentally fill in the connections that are shown in the three exhibits. Accountants assume too much.

Connecting the Dots

In my experience, most business managers and executives, and for that matter even some CPAs, do not recognize the connecting links between the financial statements that I show in Exhibits 3.1, 3.2, and 3.3. Over the years I have corresponded with many persons who have contacted me requesting the Excel workbook file of the exhibits in the book. (See the Preface for my e-mail address.) Over and over they mention one point: the value of seeing the connections between the financial statements.

I did not fully understand these connections myself until I started teaching at the University of California at Berkeley in the early 1960s. In browsing through an old, out-of-print textbook I came upon the point that financial statements, although presented separately, are *articulated* with one another. Even though I had already earned my Ph.D., I had not seen this critical point before. (Or, perhaps I slept through that particular lecture in college.) I was struck by the term "articulated." In my mind's eye I could see an articulated bus, or a bus having two compartments that were connected together.

Exhibits 3.1, 3.2, and 3.3 provide the framework for the following several chapters. Each chapter focuses on one key connection between the financial statements. Then we move on to the cash flow chapters. The connections are vital for understanding the difference between profit and cash flow from profit.

EXHIBIT 4.1—SALES REVENUE AND ACCOUNTS RECEIVABLE
Dollar Amounts in Thousands

BALANCE SHEET AT END OF YEAR

Assets

Cash	$ 3,265	
Accounts Receivable	5,000	
Inventory	8,450	
Prepaid Expenses	960	
Total Current Assets		$17,675
Property, Plant, and Equipment	$16,500	
Accumulated Depreciation	(4,250)	12,250
Goodwill	$ 7,850	
Accumulated Amortization	(2,275)	5,575
Total Assets		**$35,500**

Assuming five weeks of annual sales revenue is uncollected at year-end, the ending balance of Accounts Receivable is:

$5/52 \times \$52,000 = \$5,000$

INCOME STATEMENT FOR YEAR

Sales Revenue	$52,000
Cost of Goods Sold Expense	33,800
Gross Margin	$18,200
Operating Expenses	12,480
Depreciation Expense	785
Amortization Expense	325
Operating Earnings	$ 4,610
Interest Expense	545
Earnings before Income Tax	$ 4,065
Income Tax Expense	1,423
Net Income	$ 2,642

Liabilities and Stockholders' Equity

Accounts Payable—Inventory	$ 2,600	
Accounts Payable—Operating Expenses	720	$ 3,320
Accrued Operating Expenses	$ 1,440	
Accrued Interest Expense	75	1,515
Income Tax Payable		165
Short-Term Notes Payable		3,125
Total Current Liabilities		$ 8,125
Long-Term Notes Payable		4,250
Capital Stock	$ 8,125	
Retained Earnings	15,000	
Total Owners' Equity		23,125
Total Liabilities and Stockholders' Equity		**$35,500**

4

SALES REVENUE AND ACCOUNTS RECEIVABLE

Exploring One Link at a Time

Please refer to Exhibit 4.1 on page 26. This exhibit is taken from Exhibit 3.1 presented in Chapter 3 (page 21). Exhibit 3.1 presents the big picture; it ties together all the connections between the income statement and the balance sheet. This chapter is the first of several that focus on just one connection at a time. Only one line of connection is highlighted in Exhibit 4.1—the one between sales revenue in the income statement and accounts receivable in the balance sheet.

Exhibit 4.1 presents the company's income statement and balance sheet, but *not* its cash flow statement for the year. The connections between changes in the balance sheet accounts and the cash flow statement are explained in later chapters. Including the cash flow statement here would be a distraction.

The central idea in this and the several following chapters is that the profit-making activities reported in the income statement drive, or determine, an asset or a liability. Assets and liabilities are reported in the balance sheet. For example, the company's sales revenue for the year just ended was $52 million. Of this total sales revenue, $5 million is in the accounts receivable asset account at the end of the year. The $5 million is that part of annual sales that had not yet been collected at the end of the year.

In the following chapters we explore each linkage between an income statement account and its connecting account in the balance sheet. (Well, to be more accurate, one chapter deals with the connection between two balance sheet accounts.)

How Sales Revenue Drives Accounts Receivable

In this business example the company made $52,000,000 total sales during the year. This is a sizable amount, equal to $1,000,000 average sales revenue per week. When making a sale the total amount of the sale (sales price times quantity for all products sold) is recorded in the *sales revenue* account. This account accumulates all sales made during the year. On the first day of the year it starts with a zero balance; at the end of the last day of the year it has a $52,000,000 balance. In short, the balance in this account at year-end is the sum of all sales for the entire year (assuming all sales are recorded, of course).

In this example the business makes all its sales on credit, which means that cash is not received until sometime after the day of sale. This company sells to other businesses that demand credit. (Many retailers, such as supermarkets, make all sales for cash, or accept credit cards that are converted into cash immediately.) The amount owed to the company from making a sale on credit is immediately recorded in the *accounts receivable* asset account for the amount of each sale. Sometime later, when cash is collected from customers, the cash account is increased and the accounts receivable account is decreased.

Extending credit to customers creates a cash inflow lag. The accounts receivable balance is the amount of this lag. At year-end the balance in this asset account is the amount of uncollected sales revenue. Most of the sales made on credit during the year have been converted into cash by the end of the year. Also, the accounts receivable balance at the start of the year from sales made last year was collected. But, many sales made during the latter part of the year have not yet been collected by year-end. The total amount of these uncollected sales is found in the ending balance of accounts receivable.

Some of the company's customers pay quickly to take advantage of prompt payment discounts offered by the company. (These discounts off list prices reduce sales prices but speed up cash receipts.) On the other hand, the average customer waits 5 weeks to pay the company and forgoes the prompt payment discount. Some customers wait 10 weeks or more to pay the company, despite the company's efforts to encourage them to pay sooner. The company puts up with these slow payers because they generate a lot of repeat sales.

In sum, the company has a mix of quick, regular, and slow-paying customers. Suppose that the average credit period for all customers is 5 weeks. This means that 5 weeks of annual sales were still uncollected at year-end. (This doesn't mean every customer takes 5 weeks to pay, but rather than the average time before paying is 5 weeks.) The relationship between annual sales revenue and the ending balance of accounts receivable, therefore, can be expressed as follows:

$$\frac{5}{52} \times \begin{array}{c} \$52,000,000 \\ \text{Sales Revenue} \\ \text{for the Year} \end{array} = \begin{array}{c} \$5,000,000 \\ \text{Accounts Receivable} \\ \text{at End of Year} \end{array}$$

Exhibit 4.1 on page 26 shows that the ending balance of accounts receivable is $5,000,000.

The main point is that the average sales credit period determines the size of accounts receivable. The longer the average sales credit period, the larger is accounts receivable.

Let's approach this key point from another direction. Suppose we didn't know the average credit period. Nevertheless, using information from the financial statements we can determine the average credit period. The first step is to calculate the following ratio:

$$\frac{\$52,000,000 \text{ Sales Revenue}}{\$5,000,000 \text{ Accounts Receivable}} = 10.4 \text{ Times}$$

This calculation gives the *accounts receivable turnover ratio*, which is 10.4 in this example. Dividing this ratio into 52 weeks gives the average sales credit period expressed in number of weeks:

$$\frac{52 \text{ Weeks}}{10.4 \text{ Accounts Receivable Turnover Ratio}} = 5 \text{ Weeks}$$

Time is of the essence. What interests the business manager, and the company's creditors and investors as well, is how long it takes on average to turn accounts receivable into cash. I think the accounts receivable turnover ratio is most meaningful when it is used to determine the number of weeks (or days) it takes a company to convert its accounts receivable into cash.

You may argue that 5 weeks is too long an average sales credit period for the company. This is precisely the point: What should it be? The manager in charge has to decide whether the average credit period is getting out of hand. The manager can shorten credit terms, shut off credit to slow payers, or step up collection efforts.

This isn't the place to discuss customer credit policies relative to marketing strategies and customer relations, which would take us far beyond the field of financial accounting. But, to make an important point here, assume that without losing any sales the company's average sales credit period had been only 4 weeks, instead of 5 weeks.

In this alternative scenario the company's ending accounts receivable balance would have been $1,000,000 less ($5,000,000 ÷ 5 weeks = $1,000,000), which is the average sales revenue per week ($52,000,000 annual sales revenue ÷ 52 weeks = $1,000,000). The company would have collected $1,000,000 more cash during the year. With this additional cash inflow the company could have borrowed $1,000,000 less. At an annual 8% interest rate this would have saved the business $80,000 interest before income tax. Or, the owners could have invested $1,000,000 less in the business and put their money elsewhere.

The main point, of course, is that capital has a cost. Excess accounts receivable means that excess debt or excess owners' equity capital is being used by the business. The business is not as capital-efficient as it could be.

A slow-up in collecting customers' receivables or a deliberate shift in business policy allowing longer credit terms causes accounts receivable to increase. Additional capital would have to be secured, or the company would have to attempt to get by on a smaller cash balance.

If you were the business manager in this example you'd have to decide whether the size of accounts receivable, being

5 weeks of annual sales revenue, is consistent with your company's sales credit terms and your collection policies. Perhaps 5 weeks is too long and you need to take action. If you were a creditor or an investor in the company, you should pay attention to whether the manager is allowing the average sales credit period to get out of control. A major change in the average credit period may signal a significant change in the company's policies.

EXHIBIT 5.1—COST OF GOODS SOLD EXPENSE AND INVENTORY
Dollar Amounts in Thousands

BALANCE SHEET AT END OF YEAR		
Assets		
Cash	$ 3,265	
Accounts Receivable	5,000	
Inventory	8,450	
Prepaid Expenses	960	
Total Current Assets		$17,675
Property, Plant, and Equipment	$16,500	
Accumulated Depreciation	(4,250)	12,250
Goodwill	$ 7,850	
Accumulated Amortization	(2,275)	5,575
Total Assets		**$35,500**

Assuming the year-end inventory of goods awaiting sale equals 13 weeks of annual cost of goods sold, the ending balance of inventory is:

$13/52 \times \$33,800 = \$8,450$

INCOME STATEMENT FOR YEAR	
Sales Revenue	$52,000
Cost of Goods Sold Expense	33,800
Gross Margin	$18,200
Operating Expenses	12,480
Depreciation Expense	785
Amortization Expense	325
Operating Earnings	$ 4,610
Interest Expense	545
Earnings before Income Tax	$ 4,065
Income Tax Expense	1,423
Net Income	$ 2,642

Liabilities and Stockholders' Equity		
Accounts Payable—Inventory	$ 2,600	
Accounts Payable—Operating Expenses	720	$ 3,320
Accrued Operating Expenses	$ 1,440	
Accrued Interest Expense	75	1,515
Income Tax Payable		165
Short-Term Notes Payable		3,125
Total Current Liabilities		$ 8,125
Long-Term Notes Payable		4,250
Capital Stock	$ 8,125	
Retained Earnings	15,000	
Total Owners' Equity		23,125
Total Liabilities and Stockholders' Equity		**$35,500**

5

COST OF GOODS SOLD EXPENSE AND INVENTORY

Holding Inventory for Some Time before It's Sold

Please refer to Exhibit 5.1 on page 32. (The preceding chapter explains the format of this exhibit, which is also used in following chapters; see page 28 for review if necessary.) This chapter focuses on the connection between *cost of goods sold expense* in the income statement and *inventory* in the balance sheet. Recall that this business sells products, which are also called "goods" or "merchandise."

Cost of goods sold expense means just that—the cost of all products sold to customers during the year. The revenue from the sales is recorded in the sales revenue account, which is reported just above the cost of goods sold expense in the income statement. Cost of goods sold expense is, by far, the largest expense in the company's income statement, being almost three times its operating expenses for the year.

Subtracting cost of goods sold expense from sales revenue gives *gross margin*, which is the first profit line reported in the income statement. (Sometimes gross margin is labeled *gross profit*, but as I mention earlier in the book the term profit is generally avoided in income statements.)

The word "gross" is used to emphasize that no other expenses have been deducted. Only the cost of the products sold is deducted from sales revenue at this point in the income statement. Gross margin is the starting point for earning an adequate final, bottom-line profit for the period. In other words,

the first step is to sell products for enough gross margin so that all other expenses can be covered and still leave an adequate remainder of profit. Later chapters discuss the company's other expenses.

In this example the business earned 35% gross margin on its sales revenue (data from Exhibit 5.1):

$$\frac{\$18,200,000 \text{ Gross Margin}}{\$52,000,000 \text{ Sales Revenue}} = \begin{array}{c} 35\% \text{ Gross Margin} \\ \text{on Sales Revenue} \end{array}$$

The business sells many different products, some for more than 35% gross margin and some for less. In total, for all products sold during the year, its average gross margin is 35%—which is fairly typical for a broad cross section of businesses. Gross margins more than 50% or less than 20% are unusual; the majority of businesses fall within this range.

To sell products most businesses must have a stock of products on hand, which is called *inventory*. If a company sells products it would be a real shock to see no inventory in its balance sheet (possible, but highly unlikely). Notice in Exhibit 5.1

that the line of connection is not between sales revenue and inventory, but between cost of goods sold expense and inventory. Inventory is reported at *cost* in the balance sheet, not at its sales value.

The inventory asset account accumulates the cost of the products purchased or manufactured. Acquisition cost stays in an inventory asset account until the products are sold to customers. At this time the cost of the products is removed from inventory and charged out to cost of goods sold expense. (Products may become nonsalable or may be stolen, in which case their cost is removed from inventory and charged to cost of goods sold or to another expense.)

The company's inventory balance at year-end—$8,450,000 in this example—is the cost of products awaiting sale next year. The $33,800,000 deducted from sale revenue in the income statement is the cost of goods that were sold during the year. Of course none of these products were on hand in year-end inventory.

Some of the company's products are manufactured in a short time and some take much longer. Once the production process is finished the products are moved into its warehouse for storage until the goods are sold and delivered to customers. Some products are sold quickly, almost right off the end of the production line. Other products sit in the warehouse many weeks before being sold. This business, like most companies, sells a mix of different products—some of which have very short holding periods and some very long holding periods.

In this example the company's *average* inventory holding period for all products is 13 weeks, or three months on average. This time interval includes the production process time and the warehouse storage time. For example, a product may take 3 weeks to manufacture and then be held in storage 10 weeks, or vice versa. Internally, manufacturers separate "work-in-process" inventory (products still in the process of being manufactured) from "finished goods" (completed inventory ready for delivery to customers). Usually only one combined inventory account is reported in the external balance sheet, as shown in Exhibit 5.1.

Given that its average inventory holding period is 13 weeks, the company's inventory cost can be expressed as follows:

$$\frac{13}{52} \times \begin{array}{c} \$33,800,000 \\ \text{Cost of Goods Sold} \\ \text{Expense for Year} \end{array} = \begin{array}{c} \$8,450,000 \\ \text{Inventory} \\ \text{at End of Year} \end{array}$$

Notice in Exhibit 5.1 that the company's ending inventory balance is $8,450,000.

The main point is that the average inventory holding period determines the size of inventory relative to annual cost of goods sold. The longer the manufacturing and warehouse holding period, the larger is inventory. Business managers prefer to operate with the lowest level of inventory possible, without causing lost sales due to being out of products when customers want to buy them. A business invests substantial capital in inventory.

Now, suppose we didn't know the company's average inventory holding period. Using information from its financial statements we can determine the average inventory holding period. The first step is to calculate the following ratio:

$$\frac{\$33,800,000 \text{ Cost of Goods Sold Expense}}{\$8,450,000 \text{ Inventory}} = 4.00 \text{ Times}$$

This gives the *inventory turnover ratio*. Dividing this ratio into 52 weeks gives the average inventory holding period expressed in number of weeks:

$$\frac{52 \text{ Weeks}}{4.00 \text{ Inventory Turnover Ratio}} = 13 \text{ Weeks}$$

Time is the essence of the matter, as with the average sales credit period extended to customers. What interests the manager, as well as the company's creditors and investors, is how long the company has to hold inventory before products are sold. I think the inventory turnover ratio is most meaningful when used to determine the number of weeks (or days) that it takes before inventory is sold.

Is 13 weeks too long? Should the company's average inventory holding period be shorter? These are precisely the key questions business managers, creditors, and investors should answer. If the holding period is longer than necessary, too much capital is being tied up in inventory. Or, the company may be cash poor because it keeps too much money in inventory and not enough in the bank.

To demonstrate this key point, suppose the company with better inventory management could have reduced its average inventory holding period to, say, 10 weeks. This would have been a rather dramatic improvement, to say the least. But modern inventory management techniques such as just-in-time (JIT) promise such improvement. If the company had reduced its average inventory holding period to just 10 weeks its ending inventory would have been:

$$\begin{array}{c}\$650,000 \text{ Cost of} \\ \text{Goods Sold per Week}\end{array} \times 10 \text{ Weeks} = \begin{array}{c}\$6,500,000 \\ \text{Ending Inventory}\end{array}$$

In this scenario ending inventory would be $1,950,000 less ($8,450,000 versus $6,500,000). The company would have needed $1,950,000 less capital, or would have had this much more cash balance at its disposal.

However, with only 10 weeks' inventory the company may be unable to make some sales because certain products might not be available for immediate delivery to customers. In other words, if overall inventory is too low, *stock-outs* may occur. Nothing is more frustrating, especially to sales staff, than having willing customers but no products to deliver to them. The cost of carrying inventory has to be balanced against the profit opportunities lost by not having products on hand ready for sale.

In summary, business managers, creditors, and investors should watch that the inventory holding period is neither too high nor too low. If too high, capital is being wasted; if too low, profit opportunities are being missed. Comparisons of a company's inventory holding period with those of its competitors and with historical trends provide useful benchmarks.

National trade associations and organizations collect inventory and other financial data from their members that is published in their journals or that is available at relatively low cost. The federal Department of Commerce and Small Business Administration are useful sources of benchmark information. Also, a company's banker or loan officer is usually a good person to ask about typical inventory practices for a line of business.

EXHIBIT 6.1—INVENTORY AND ACCOUNTS PAYABLE
Dollar Amounts in Thousands

INCOME STATEMENT FOR YEAR

Sales Revenue	$52,000
Cost of Goods Sold Expense	33,800
Gross Margin	$18,200
Operating Expenses	12,480
Depreciation Expense	785
Amortization Expense	325
Operating Earnings	$ 4,610
Interest Expense	545
Earnings before Income Tax	$ 4,065
Income Tax Expense	1,423
Net Income	$ 2,642

Assuming the amount payable at year-end for inventory related purchases is 4 weeks of the 13 weeks in inventory, the year-end balance of Accounts Payable for inventory is:

$4/13 \times \$8,450 = \$2,600$

BALANCE SHEET AT END OF YEAR

Assets

Cash	$ 3,265	
Accounts Receivable	5,000	
Inventory	8,450	
Prepaid Expenses	960	
Total Current Assets		$17,675
Property, Plant, and Equipment	$16,500	
Accumulated Depreciation	(4,250)	12,250
Goodwill	$ 7,850	
Accumulated Amortization	(2,275)	5,575
Total Assets		**$35,500**

Liabilities and Stockholders' Equity

Accounts Payable—Inventory	$ 2,600	
Accounts Payable—Operating Expenses	720	$ 3,320
Accrued Operating Expenses	$ 1,440	
Accrued Interest Expense	75	1,515
Income Tax Payable		165
Short-Term Notes Payable		3,125
Total Current Liabilities		$ 8,125
Long-Term Notes Payable		4,250
Capital Stock	$ 8,125	
Retained Earnings	15,000	
Total Owners' Equity		23,125
Total Liabilities and Stockholders' Equity		**$35,500**

6

INVENTORY AND ACCOUNTS PAYABLE

Acquiring Inventory on Credit

Please refer to Exhibit 6.1 on page 38. This chapter focuses on the connection between the *inventory* asset account in the balance sheet and one of the *accounts payable* liabilities in the balance sheet.

Notice that we are looking at a connection between balance sheet accounts; the previous two chapters connect an income statement account with a balance sheet account. The linkage explained in this chapter is different; it's not about how sales revenue or an expense drives an asset, but rather how inventory drives a corresponding liability.

The company in this example is a manufacturer, which means it makes the products it sells. To begin, the company purchases raw materials needed in its production process. These purchases are made on credit; the company doesn't pay for these purchases right away. Also, other production inputs are bought on credit. For example, once a month the public utility sends a bill for the gas and electricity used during the month. The company takes several weeks before paying its utility bills. The company purchases several other manufacturing inputs on credit also.

In the company's balance sheet (see Exhibit 6.1) the liability for its various production-related purchases on credit is presented in *accounts payable—inventory* (see page 38). The company's operating expenses also generate accounts payable; these are shown in a second accounts payable liability account (discussed in Chapter 7).

The company's inventory holding period is much longer than its purchase credit period (which is typical for most businesses). In other words, accounts payable are paid much sooner than inventory is sold. In this example, the company's inventory holding period from start of the production process to final sale averages 13 weeks (as explained in Chapter 5). But the company pays its accounts payable after 4 weeks, on average.

Some purchases are paid for quickly, to take advantage of prompt payment discounts offered by vendors. But the business takes 6 weeks or longer to pay many other bills. Based on its experience and policies, a business knows the average purchase credit period for its production-related purchases. In this example, suppose it takes 4 weeks on average to pay these liabilities. Therefore, the year-end balance of accounts payable—inventory can be expressed as follows:

$$\frac{4}{13} \times \frac{\$8,450,000}{\text{Inventory}} = \frac{\$2,600,000}{\text{Accounts Payable—Inventory}}$$

In short, this liability equals $4/13$ of the inventory balance. The business gets a "free ride" for the first 4 weeks of holding inventory, because it waits this long before paying for its purchases on credit. But the remaining 9 weeks of the inventory holding period has to be financed from its debt and stockholders' equity sources of capital.

Economists are fond of saying that "there's no such thing as a free lunch." So, calling the 4 weeks delay in paying for purchases on credit a free ride is not entirely accurate. Sellers that extend credit set their prices slightly higher to compensate for the delay in receiving cash from their customers. In other words, a small but hidden interest charge is built into the cost paid by the purchaser.

EXHIBIT 7.1—OPERATING EXPENSES AND ACCOUNTS PAYABLE
Dollar Amounts in Thousands

INCOME STATEMENT FOR YEAR

Sales Revenue	$52,000
Cost of Goods Sold Expense	33,800
Gross Margin	$18,200
Operating Expenses	12,480
Depreciation Expense	785
Amortization Expense	325
Operating Earnings	$ 4,610
Interest Expense	545
Earnings before Income Tax	$ 4,065
Income Tax Expense	1,423
Net Income	$ 2,642

> Assuming 3 weeks of annual operating expenses are unpaid at the end of the year, the year-end balance of Accounts Payable for operating expenses is:
>
> 3/52 × $12,480 = $720

BALANCE SHEET AT END OF YEAR

Assets

Cash	$ 3,265	
Accounts Receivable	5,000	
Inventory	8,450	
Prepaid Expenses	960	
Total Current Assets		$17,675
Property, Plant, and Equipment	$16,500	
Accumulated Depreciation	(4,250)	12,250
Goodwill	$ 7,850	
Accumulated Amortization	(2,275)	5,575
Total Assets		$35,500

Liabilities and Stockholders' Equity

Accounts Payable—Inventory	$ 2,600	
Accounts Payable—Operating Expenses	720	$ 3,320
Accrued Operating Expenses	$ 1,440	
Accrued Interest Expense	75	1,515
Income Tax Payable		165
Short-Term Notes Payable		3,125
Total Current Liabilities		$ 8,125
Long-Term Notes Payable		4,250
Capital Stock	$ 8,125	
Retained Earnings	15,000	
Total Owners' Equity		23,125
Total Liabilities and Stockholders' Equity		$35,500

7

OPERATING EXPENSES
AND ACCOUNTS PAYABLE

Recording Operating Expenses before They Are Paid

Please refer to Exhibit 7.1 on page 42, which highlights the connection between *operating expenses* in the income statement and *accounts payable—operating expenses* in the balance sheet. This chapter explains how operating expenses drives this particular liability of a business.

Day in and day out many operating expenses are recorded when they are paid, at which time an expense is increased and cash is decreased. But some operating expenses have to be recorded *before* they are paid—which is the focus of this chapter.

"Operating expenses" is a catchall title that groups together many different specific expenses of running (operating) a business enterprise. In this example the annual depreciation expense on the company's long-lived, fixed assets is shown as a separate expense, as is the annual amortization expense; the $12,480,000 total operating expenses in the income statement does not include depreciation or amortization expense. The operating expenses account also excludes interest expense and income tax expense, which are reported separately in the income statement.

Included under the umbrella of operating expenses are the following specific expenses (in no particular order):

- Rental of buildings, copiers, computers, telephone system equipment, and various other assets.

- Wages, salaries, commissions, bonuses, and other compensation paid managers, office staff, salespersons, warehouse workers, security guards, and other employees. (Compensation paid production employees is included in cost of goods manufactured, not in operating expenses.)

- Payroll taxes and several fringe benefit costs of labor, such as health and medical plan contributions and employee retirement plan costs.

- Office and data processing supplies.

- Telephone, fax, Internet, and web site costs.

- Inventory shrinkage due to shoplifting and employee theft or careless handling and storage of products; the cost of goods stolen and damaged may be written off to cost of goods sold expense or, alternatively, included in operating expenses.

- Liability, fire, accident, and other insurance costs.

- Advertising and sales promotion costs, which are major expenditures by many businesses.

- Bad debts, which are past-due accounts receivable that turn out to be not collectible and have to be written off.

- Transportation and shipping costs.

- Travel and entertainment costs.

Even relatively small businesses keep 50 to 100 separate accounts for specific operating expenses. Larger business corporations keep thousands of specific expense accounts. In their *external* financial reports, however, publicly owned corporations report only one, two, or three operating expenses. For instance, advertising expenses are reported internally to managers, but you don't always see this particular expense reported separately in external income statements.

Actually, grouping operating expenses (except for depreciation and amortization) into one collective account is rather convenient here. Operating expenses are recorded in just four basic ways. One way is to record expenses when they are paid—not before, nor after. This chapter explains another basic way operating expenses are recorded—by increasing a liability called "accounts payable—operating expenses." (Following chapters explain the other two basic ways of recording operating expenses and the asset and liability accounts involved.)

It would be a simple world if every dollar of operating expenses were a dollar actually paid out in the same period. But business is not so simple, as this and later chapters demonstrate. The point is that for many operating expenses a business cannot wait to record the expense until it pays the expense. As soon as a liability is incurred the amount of expense has to be recorded.

A liability is incurred when a company takes on an obligation to make future payment and has received the economic benefit of the cost in operating the business. Recording this sort of liability is one fundamental aspect of the *accrual basis* of accounting. Expenses are recorded before they are paid so that the amount of the expense is deducted from sales revenue to measure profit for the period.

For example, suppose on December 15 a business receives in the mail a bill from its attorneys for legal work done for the company over the previous two or three months. The company's accounting (fiscal) year ends December 31. The company will not pay its lawyers until next year. This cost belongs in this year, and should be recorded in the legal fees expense account. So, the company records an increase in the accounts payable liability account to record the legal expense.

This is just one example of many; other examples include bills from newspapers for advertisements that have already appeared in the papers, telephone bills, and so on. Generally speaking these liabilities have fairly short credit periods.

Based on its experience, a business should know the average time it takes to pay its short-term accounts payable. The average credit period of the company in our example is 3 weeks. Thus, the amount of its accounts payable—operating expenses can be expressed as follows:

$$\frac{3}{52} \times \begin{matrix} \$12,480,000 \\ \text{Operating Expenses} \\ \text{for Year} \end{matrix} = \begin{matrix} \$720,000 \\ \text{Accounts Payable—} \\ \text{Operating Expenses} \end{matrix}$$

In Exhibit 7.1 notice that the year-end balance of this liability account is $720,000.

Operating costs that are not paid right away are recorded in accounts payable both to recognize the obligation of the business to make payment for these costs and to record expenses that have benefited the operations of the business, so that profit is measured correctly for the period. In other words, there's both an income statement and a balance sheet reason for recording unpaid expenses.

Generally accepted accounting principles (GAAP) require that accounts payable be recorded for expenses that haven't been paid by the end of the accounting year. However, the recording of unpaid expenses does *not* decrease cash. Cash outflow occurs later, when the accounts payable are paid. Chapter 13 looks into the cash flow analysis of making profit.

EXHIBIT 8.1—OPERATING EXPENSES AND PREPAID EXPENSES
Dollar Amounts in Thousands

INCOME STATEMENT FOR YEAR

Sales Revenue	$52,000
Cost of Goods Sold Expense	33,800
Gross Margin	$18,200
Operating Expenses	12,480
Depreciation Expense	785
Amortization Expense	325
Operating Earnings	$ 4,610
Interest Expense	545
Earnings before Income Tax	$ 4,065
Income Tax Expense	1,423
Net Income	$ 2,642

Assuming the business has paid certain costs that will not be recorded as expenses until next year that in total equal 4 weeks of its annual operating expenses, the year-end balance of Prepaid Expenses is:

$$4/52 \times \$12,480 = \$960$$

BALANCE SHEET AT END OF YEAR

Assets

Cash	$ 3,265	
Accounts Receivable	5,000	
Inventory	8,450	
Prepaid Expenses	960	
Total Current Assets		$17,675
Property, Plant, and Equipment	$16,500	
Accumulated Depreciation	(4,250)	12,250
Goodwill	$ 7,850	
Accumulated Amortization	(2,275)	5,575
Total Assets		$35,500

Liabilities and Stockholders' Equity

Accounts Payable—Inventory	$ 2,600	
Accounts Payable—Operating Expenses	720	$ 3,320
Accrued Operating Expenses	$ 1,440	
Accrued Interest Expense	75	1,515
Income Tax Payable		165
Short-Term Notes Payable		3,125
Total Current Liabilities		$ 8,125
Long-Term Notes Payable		4,250
Capital Stock	$ 8,125	
Retained Earnings	15,000	
Total Owners' Equity		23,125
Total Liabilities and Stockholders' Equity		$35,500

8

OPERATING EXPENSES AND PREPAID EXPENSES

Paying Operating Costs *before*
They Are Recorded as Expenses

To begin please refer to Exhibit 8.1 on page 46, which highlights the connection between *operating expenses* in the income statement and *prepaid expenses* in the balance sheet. This chapter explains that operating expenses drive this particular asset of a business.

Chapter 7 explains that some operating expenses are recorded before they are paid—by recording a liability for unpaid expenses. This chapter, in contrast, explains that certain costs are paid *before* these amounts should be recorded as operating expenses.

A good example of prepaid expenses is insurance premiums that must be paid in advance of the insurance policy period—which usually covers 6 or 12 months. Another example is office and computer supplies bought in bulk and then gradually used up over several weeks. Annual property taxes may be paid at the start of the tax year; these amounts should be allocated over all the months covered by the property taxes.

Cash outlays for paid-in-advance costs are put in a holding account and then the amounts are gradually charged out over time to operating expenses. Doing this is the means of deferring or delaying the expensing of costs to future periods. The account used for this purpose is called *prepaid expenses*. The cost is allocated so that each future month receives its fair share of the cost. Every month an entry is recorded to remove the appropriate fraction of the cost from the prepaid expenses account, and to record this portion in an operating expense account.

Based on its experience and the nature of its operations, a business knows how large, on average, its prepaid expenses are relative to its annual operating expenses. In this example the company's prepaid expenses balance is 4 weeks of its annual operating expenses. Thus, its prepaid expenses can be expressed as follows:

$$\frac{4}{52} \times \overset{\$12,480,000}{\underset{\text{for Year}}{\text{Operating Expenses}}} = \overset{\$960,000}{\underset{\text{Expenses}}{\text{Prepaid}}}$$

In Exhibit 8.1 notice that the year-end balance of this asset account is \$960,000, which is much smaller than the company's accounts receivable and inventory balances. (This is typical for most businesses.)

Operating costs that are paid in advance are put in prepaid expenses both to recognize the prepayment of these costs and to delay recording the expense until the proper time, so that profit is measured correctly for each period. In other words, there's both an income statement and a balance sheet reason for recording prepaid expenses. Charging off prepayments immediately to operating expenses would be premature—there would be a robbing Paul (expenses higher this period) to pay Peter (expenses lower next period) effect on profit.

Generally accepted accounting principles (GAAP) demand that operating costs paid in advance must be put in the prepaid expenses asset account, and not charged to expense immediately (assuming the amounts are material, or sizable enough to make a difference). The prepayment of operating expenses decreases cash, of course. Cash outflow takes place this year, even though the expense won't show up until next year. Chapter 13 looks into the cash flow analysis of making profit.

EXHIBIT 9.1—DEPRECIATION AND AMORTIZATION EXPENSES FOR USING LONG-TERM OPERATING ASSETS
Dollar Amounts in Thousands

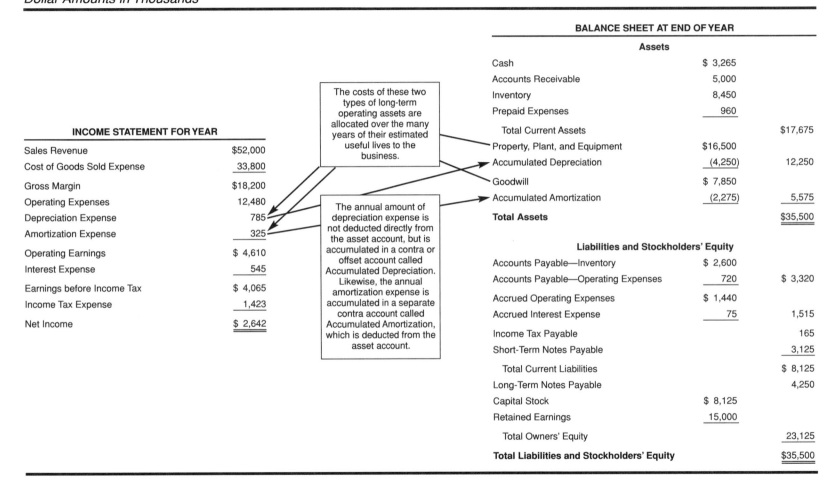

INCOME STATEMENT FOR YEAR

Sales Revenue	$52,000
Cost of Goods Sold Expense	33,800
Gross Margin	$18,200
Operating Expenses	12,480
Depreciation Expense	785
Amortization Expense	325
Operating Earnings	$ 4,610
Interest Expense	545
Earnings before Income Tax	$ 4,065
Income Tax Expense	1,423
Net Income	$ 2,642

The costs of these two types of long-term operating assets are allocated over the many years of their estimated useful lives to the business.

The annual amount of depreciation expense is not deducted directly from the asset account, but is accumulated in a contra or offset account called Accumulated Depreciation. Likewise, the annual amortization expense is accumulated in a separate contra account called Accumulated Amortization, which is deducted from the asset account.

BALANCE SHEET AT END OF YEAR

Assets

Cash	$ 3,265	
Accounts Receivable	5,000	
Inventory	8,450	
Prepaid Expenses	960	
Total Current Assets		$17,675
Property, Plant, and Equipment	$16,500	
Accumulated Depreciation	(4,250)	12,250
Goodwill	$ 7,850	
Accumulated Amortization	(2,275)	5,575
Total Assets		$35,500

Liabilities and Stockholders' Equity

Accounts Payable—Inventory	$ 2,600	
Accounts Payable—Operating Expenses	720	$ 3,320
Accrued Operating Expenses	$ 1,440	
Accrued Interest Expense	75	1,515
Income Tax Payable		165
Short-Term Notes Payable		3,125
Total Current Liabilities		$ 8,125
Long-Term Notes Payable		4,250
Capital Stock	$ 8,125	
Retained Earnings	15,000	
Total Owners' Equity		23,125
Total Liabilities and Stockholders' Equity		$35,500

9

LONG-TERM OPERATING ASSETS: DEPRECIATION AND AMORTIZATION EXPENSE

Brief Review of Expense Accounting

By now you should have a basic sense of *accrual-based* expense accounting. Cash outlays for operating a business are not necessarily recorded to expense in the same period the cash disbursement takes place. In other words, expenses are not recorded on a simple cash basis of accounting, where all a business needs to do is to keep track of the checks it writes.

Rather, financial accounting is mainly concerned with the correct timing of expenses—to match expenses with sales revenue or to match expenses with the correct period if there is no direct association between an expense and sales revenue. Each basis for recording expenses is explained briefly here:

- *Matching Expenses with Sales Revenue:* Cost of goods sold expense, sales commissions expense, and any other expense directly connected with making particular sales are recorded in the same period as the sales revenue. This is straightforward enough; without a doubt all direct expenses of making sales should be matched against sales revenue. You agree, don't you?

- *Matching Expenses with the Correct Period:* Many expenses are not directly identifiable with particular sales, such as office employees' salaries, rental of warehouse space, computer processing and accounting costs, legal and audit fees, interest on borrowed money, and many more. Nondirect expenses are

just as necessary as direct expenses. But, there's no objective or clear-cut way to match nondirect expenses with particular sales. Therefore, nondirect expenses are recorded to the period in which the benefit to the business occurs.

The recording of expenses involves the use of asset and liability accounts. Chapter 5 explains the use of the inventory account to hold back the cost of products that are manufactured or purchased until the goods are sold, at which time cost of goods expense is recorded. Chapter 7 explains the use of the accounts payable liability account for recording unpaid costs that should be recorded as expenses in the period. And, Chapter 8 explains the use of the prepaid expenses asset account to delay or defer the recording of operating expenses until the proper time.

This chapter explains that the costs of long-lived operating assets of a business are spread out over their useful lives. The allocation of the cost of a long-term operating asset is called *depreciation* for tangible assets and *amortization* for intangible assets. Please be careful: Depreciation is confusing to many people. Many persons think it refers to the loss of value, or decline in market value of an asset such as a personal automobile. This notion is not entirely wrong, but in financial accounting depreciation means *cost allocation*.

Depreciation Expense

Please see Exhibit 9.1 on page 50 that shows the connections between two expenses of the business—*depreciation* and *amortization*—and their respective assets in the balance sheet. In brief, the costs of these two assets are allocated over their estimated economic lives, and the annual expense is accumulated in a separate offset account that is deducted from the cost of the assets. The logic and methods of recording depreciation and amortization expenses are explained in this chapter.

The company in this example uses certain specialized machinery, equipment, and tools that are rented under various lease contracts. The rents paid on these particular assets are charged to operating expenses. Leased assets are not reported in a company's balance sheet (unless the lease is essentially a method to finance the purchase of the asset). The business doesn't own leased (rented) assets. However, the rental commitments under long-term leases are disclosed in the footnotes to the balance sheet.

In contrast, the company owns most of its fixed assets—a warehouse and office building, office furniture and fixtures, computers, delivery trucks, forklifts used in the warehouse, and automobiles used by its salespersons. The business buys these assets, uses them several years, and eventually disposes of them.

The long-term tangible operating assets owned by a business usually are grouped into one inclusive account for balance sheet reporting. One common title is "property, plant and equipment." (A detailed breakdown of fixed assets may be disclosed in a foot-note to the financial statements, or in a separate schedule.) At the end of its most recent year the business reports property, plant and equipment at $16,500,000—see Exhibit 9.1. This amount is the *original cost* of its fixed assets, which is how much they cost when the business bought them.

Fixed assets are used several years, but eventually they wear out and lose their utility to a business. In short, these assets have a limited life span—they don't last forever. For example, delivery trucks may be driven 150,000 or 200,000 miles, but they have to be replaced eventually.

The cost of a delivery truck, for instance, is prorated over the years of expected use to the business. How many years, exactly? A business has its experience to go on in estimating the useful lives of fixed assets. In theory, a business should make the best forecast for how long each fixed asset will be used, and then spread its cost over this life span. However, theory doesn't count for much on this score. Most businesses turn to the federal income tax code; it provides guidelines of useful lives for fixed assets that are allowed for determining depreciation expense in federal income tax returns.

In the income tax code every kind of fixed asset is given a minimum life over which its cost can be depreciated. The cost of land is not depreciated, on grounds that land never wears out and has a perpetual life. (Of course, the market value of a parcel of real estate can fluctuate over time; and, land can be destroyed by floods and earthquakes—but that's another matter.)

The federal income tax law permits accelerated depreciation methods. The term "accelerated"means two different things. First, the income tax law allows fixed assets to be depreciated over lives that are shorter than their actual useful lives. For example, autos and light trucks can be depreciated over five years. But these fixed assets last longer than five years (except perhaps taxicabs in New York City). Buildings placed in service after 1993 can be depreciated over 39 years, but most buildings stand longer. In writing the income tax law Congress has decided that allowing businesses to depreciate their fixed assets faster than they actually wear out is good economic policy.

Second, "accelerated" means *front-loaded*; more of the cost of a fixed asset is deducted in the first half of its useful life than in its second half. Instead of a level, uniform amount of depreciation expense year to year (which is called the *straight-line* method), the income tax law allows a business to deduct higher amounts of depreciation in the front years and less in the back years.

Accelerated depreciation permits a business to reduce its taxable income in the early years of using fixed assets. But these effects don't necessarily mean it's the best depreciation method in theory or in actual practice. In any case, accelerated depreciation methods, with the imprimatur of the income tax code, are very popular, as you may know.

A business must maintain a depreciation schedule for each of its fixed assets and keep track of original cost and how much depreciation expense is recorded each year. Only cost can be depreciated. Once the total cost of a fixed asset has been depreciated, no more depreciation expense can be recorded. At this point the fixed asset is fully depreciated even though it still may be used several more years.

In this example, the depreciation expense for the company's most recent year is $785,000—see Exhibit 9.1. Its warehouse and office building is depreciated by the straight-line method; its other fixed assets (e.g., trucks, computers, etc.) are depreciated according to an accelerated method. These two depreciation methods are compared in Chapter 21.

The amount of depreciation expense charged to each year is quite arbitrary compared with most other expenses. One reason is that useful life estimates are arbitrary. For a six-month insurance policy, there's little doubt that the total premium cost should be allocated over exactly six months. But long-lived assets such as office desks, display shelving, file cabinets, computers, and so on present much more difficult problems. Past experience is a good guide but leaves much room for error.

Given the inherent problems of estimating useful lives, financial statement readers are well advised to keep in mind the consequences of adopting conservative useful life estimates. If useful life estimates are too short (the assets really last longer), then depreciation expense is recorded too quickly. As a matter of fact, useful life estimates generally are too short. So keep this in mind.

Accountants, with the blessing of the Internal Revenue Code, take a very conservative approach. Rather than depreciate fixed assets one way for income tax and use a more realistic way for financial reporting, most businesses follow the income tax methods in their financial statements—although not in all cases. What you see in financial statements, in general, is a carbon copy of the depreciation methods used in a company's income tax returns. Is this good accounting? I have my doubts. But rapid (accelerated) depreciation is a fact of business life.

An Unusual Account—Accumulated Depreciation

The amount of depreciation expense each period is *not* recorded as a decrease in the account of the asset bing depreciated. Decreasing the asset account would seem to make sense because the whole point of depreciation is to recognize the wearing out of the asset over time. So why not decrease the asset account?

Well, the standard practice throughout the accounting world is to accumulate depreciation expense amounts in a second, companion account which is called *accumulated depreciation*. This account does what its name implies—it accumulates period-by-period the amounts charged to depreciation expense. In Exhibit 9.1 notice that the balance in this account at the end of the company's most recent year is $4,250,000.

Relative to the $16,500,000 original cost of its fixed assets the accumulated depreciation balance suggests that the company's fixed assets are not very old. Also, the company recorded $785,000 depreciation expense in its most recent year. At this clip a little over five years' depreciation has been recorded on its property, plant and equipment.

In any case, the balance in accumulated depreciation is deducted from the original cost of fixed assets. Notice in Exhibit 9.1 that cost less accumulated depreciation is $12,250,000. This amount is the portion of original cost that has not yet been depreciated; it is called the *book value* of fixed assets. Generally the entire cost of a fixed asset is depreciated. Therefore, book value represents future depreciation expense, although a business may dispose of some of its fixed assets before they are fully depreciated.

Please be clear on one point: The $4,250,000 accumulated depreciation balance is the total depreciation that has been recorded all years the fixed assets have been used. It's not just the depreciation expense from the most recent year.

Book Values versus Current Replacement Values

After several years the original cost of a company's fixed (long-term operating) assets may be quite low compared with the current replacement costs of the same assets. Although true enough, this general observation does not apply to assets that have become obsolete and would not be replaced with the same new asset. In any case, inflation is the norm in our economy. If—and this is a very hypothetical if—a company's fixed assets had to be replaced with exactly the same new fixed assets, a business would have to pay higher costs today that it did when it bought the fixed assets years ago.

The original costs of fixed assets reported in a balance sheet are not meant to be indicators of the current replacement costs of the assets. Rather, original costs are the amounts of capital invested in the assets that should be recovered through sales revenue over the years from using the assets. In other words, depreciation accounting is a cost-recovery-based method—not a "mark-to-market" method. Accounting for fixed assets does not attempt to record changes in current replacement cost.

Accountants assume, quite correctly, that the purpose of investing capital in fixed assets is that these economic resources help a business generate future sales revenue, and that the main objective is to match the cost of fixed assets against sales revenue period by period, in order to measure profit. Depreciation is one main element of the *historical cost basis* of accounting. The failure to report current replacement costs of fixed assets is of-

ten criticized by academic economists as being a major shortcoming of financial accounting. Baloney! These assets are held for use, not for sale. Economists have never managed a business, evidently.

Now I should point out that business managers do have to pay attention to the current replacement values of their fixed assets, especially for insurance purposes. Fixed assets can be destroyed or damaged by fire, flooding, riots, tornadoes, explosions, and structural failure. Quite clearly business managers should be concerned about insuring fixed assets for their current replacement costs. Indeed, insurance companies require this. However, for financial reporting purposes a business should not write up the recorded value of its fixed assets to reflect current replacement costs. This would violate generally accepted accounting principles (GAAP), which are the bedrock that financial statements rest on.

The current replacement cost argument for reporting long-term (fixed) operating assets in external financial statements and for basing depreciation expense on the current replacement cost of fixed assets has many die-hard advocates. You often see criticism of financial accounting on grounds that depreciation expense is based on historical cost. I don't think many people take this criticism seriously. Someday Congress may consider changing the income tax law to allow replacement-cost-basis depreciation (without taxing the gain from writing up fixed assets to their higher replacement costs). But, fat chance of this, in my opinion!

On the other hand, I must admit that anything is possible regarding fixed-asset depreciation within the federal income tax law. For instance, I would not be surprised if Congress were to change the useful lives of fixed assets for tax purposes—which they have done several times in the past. So far, Congress has not been willing to abandon the cost basis for fixed-asset depreciation.

Intangible Assets and Amortization Expense

Many businesses invest in *intangible* assets, which are assets that have no physical existence and that you can't see but that may be vital for the profit-making ability of the company. For example, a business may purchase the rights to a valuable patent that it will use in its production operations over many years. Or a business may buy an established trademark that is well known among consumers. When a business buys patents or trademarks the cost of these particular assets are recorded in long-term operating asset accounts called "Patents" or "Trademarks."

Instead of buying particular, specific intangible assets, a business may purchase another business as a whole and pay more than the sum of its identifiable assets. Often the company to be acquired has been in business for many years and it has built up a trusted name and reputation. It may have a large list of loyal customers that will continue to buy the company's products in the future. The experience and loyalty of the acquired company's employees may be another reason to pay for more than just the identifiable assets being acquired in the purchase of the business. Or the business being bought out may have secret processes and product formulas that give it a strong competitive advantage.

In short, there are many reasons to pay more for an established, going-concern business that just the sum of its identifiable assets. When a business pays more than the sum of the specific assets of the business being acquired, the excess amount is generally assigned to the asset account called *goodwill*. Notice in Exhibit 9.1

that the business in this example has over the years purchased goodwill for a total original cost of $7,850,000. Basically, the business has grown over the years by acquiring several other businesses and in doing so has paid more for these companies that just the total of their identifiable assets.

The cost of goodwill is, like the cost of tangible fixed assets (except land), written off to expense over the predicted useful economic lives of the goodwill. Likewise, the cost of other intangible assets, such as patents and trademarks, is written off over their predicted useful lives to the business.

The gradual write-off period by period of the cost of intangible assets is called *amortization*. At one time the maximum period for the write-off of the cost of intangibles was 40 years. Recently, however, the accounting standard was changed, and businesses now don't necessarily have to write off the cost of their intangibles. They do have to make a yearly assessment whether these intangible assets that are not being amortized have been impaired and, if so, make a write-down entry for the effect of impairment.

The business in this example writes off the cost of all its various goodwill purchases over their estimated useful lives. The total amount of these write-offs is reported as amortization expense in the income statement. See in Exhibit 9.1 that $325,000 amortization expense is reported for the year just ended. The amount recorded as amortization expense is not deducted from the asset account, but is instead put in the accumulated amortization account. This, like the accumulated depreciation account, is a contra account against the goodwill asset account. Notice in Exhibit 9.1 that the $2,275,000 balance in the accumulated amortization account is deducted from the cost of goodwill.

Financial reporting practices for intangible assets vary more compared with long-term tangible fixed assets. For example, only the net amount of cost less accumulated amortization may be disclosed in the balance sheet. In this example that would mean that only the $5,575,000 would be presented in the balance sheet (original cost less accumulated amortization).

EXHIBIT 10.1—ACCRUING UNPAID OPERATING EXPENSES AND UNPAID INTEREST EXPENSE

Dollar Amounts in Thousands

BALANCE SHEET AT END OF YEAR

Assets

Cash	$ 3,265	
Accounts Receivable	5,000	
Inventory	8,450	
Prepaid Expenses	960	
Total Current Assets		$17,675
Property, Plant, and Equipment	$16,500	
Accumulated Depreciation	(4,250)	12,250
Goodwill	$ 7,850	
Accumulated Amortization	(2,275)	5,575
Total Assets		$35,500

INCOME STATEMENT FOR YEAR

Sales Revenue	$52,000
Cost of Goods Sold Expense	33,800
Gross Margin	$18,200
Operating Expenses	12,480
Depreciation Expense	785
Amortization Expense	325
Operating Earnings	$ 4,610
Interest Expense	545
Earnings before Income Tax	$ 4,065
Income Tax Expense	1,423
Net Income	$ 2,642

> Assuming 6 weeks of annual operating expenses is unpaid at year-end, the ending balance of Accounts Payable for operating expenses is:
>
> $6/52 \times \$12{,}480 = \$1{,}440$

> A small amount of the annual interest expense is unpaid at year-end, which is recorded in the Accrued Interest Expense liability account.

Liabilities and Stockholders' Equity

Accounts Payable—Inventory	$ 2,600	
Accounts Payable—Operating Expenses	720	$ 3,320
Accrued Operating Expenses	$ 1,440	
Accrued Interest Expense	75	1,515
Income Tax Payable		165
Short-Term Notes Payable		3,125
Total Current Liabilities		$ 8,125
Long-Term Notes Payable		4,250
Capital Stock	$ 8,125	
Retained Earnings	15,000	
Total Owners' Equity		23,125
Total Liabilities and Stockholders' Equity		$35,500

10

ACCRUING UNPAID OPERATING EXPENSES AND INTEREST EXPENSE

Recording Liabilities for Certain Operating Expenses That Are Not Accounts Payable

Please refer to Exhibit 10.1 (page 60), which highlights the connection between *operating expenses* in the income statement and *accrued operating expenses* in the balance sheet, and between *interest expense* in the income statement and *accrued interest expense* in the balance sheet. You get two for the price of one in this chapter. Both connections are based on the same idea—unpaid expenses are recorded so that the full, correct amount of expense is recognized when it should be for measuring profit.

Chapter 7 explains that a business records expenses as soon as bills (invoices) are received for operating costs, even though it doesn't pay the bills until weeks later. This chapter explains that a business has to go looking for certain unpaid expenses at the end of the period. No bills or invoices are received for these expenses; they build up, or accumulate over time.

For instance, the business in our example pays its salespersons commissions based on sales prices. Commissions are calculated at the end of each month, and paid the following month. At year-end the total commissions earned for the last month of the year have not been paid. To record this expense, the company makes an entry in the liability account called *accrued operating expenses*, which is a different liability from accounts payable.

The accountant should know which expenses accumulate over time and make the appropriate calculations for these unpaid amounts at year-end. A business does not receive an invoice for these expenses from an outside vendor or supplier. A business has to generate its own internal invoices to itself, as it were; its accounting department must be especially alert to which specific operating expenses need to be accrued.

In addition to sales commissions payable, a business has several other accrued expenses payable that need to be recorded at the end of the period; the following are typical examples:

- Accumulated vacation and sick leave pay owed to employees, which can add up to a sizable amount.

- Partial-month telephone and electricity costs that have been incurred but not yet billed to the company.

- Interest on debt that hasn't come due by year-end, but the money has been borrowed for several weeks or months and interest is piling up.

- Property taxes that should be charged to the year, but the business has not received the tax assessment bill by the end of the year.

- Warranty and guarantee work on products already sold that will be done next year; the sales revenue has been recorded this year, and so these post-sale expenses also should be recorded in the same period.

Failure to record accumulated liabilities for unpaid expenses could cause serious errors in a company's annual financial statements—liabilities would be understated in its ending balance sheet and expenses would be understated for the year. A business definitely should identify which expenses accumulate over time and record the amounts of these liabilities at the end of the year.

In this example, the company's average gestation period before paying certain of its operating expenses is 6 weeks. Thus, the amount of its accrued operating expenses at year-end can be expressed as follows:

$$\frac{6}{52} \times \begin{matrix} \$12,480,000 \\ \text{Operating Expenses} \\ \text{for Year} \end{matrix} = \begin{matrix} \$1,440,000 \\ \text{Accrued Operating} \\ \text{Expenses} \end{matrix}$$

See in Exhibit 10.1 that the ending balance of accrued operating expenses is $1,440,000. Is 6 weeks high or low for a typical business? Neither, I'd say—6 weeks is more or less common, keeping in mind that every business is somewhat different. Also, I should mention that it's not unusual to see accrued operating expenses larger than a company's accounts payable for operating expenses.

Speaking of accounts payable, some businesses merge accrued operating expenses with accounts payable and report only one liability in their external balance sheets. Both types of liabilities are non-interest-bearing. They emerge out of the operations of the business, and from manufacturing or purchasing products. For this reason they are called *spontaneous liabilities*, which means they arise on the spot, not from borrowing money but from the operations of a business. Grouping both types of liabilities in one account is tolerated by generally accepted accounting principles (GAAP).

The sum of its ending $720,000 accounts payable for operating expenses and its $1,440,000 accrued operating expenses is $2,160,000. This means the business was relieved of paying this much cash during the year for its operating expenses. (Of course, the money will have to be paid next year.) The sizes of accounts payable and accrued expenses have significant impacts on cash flow, which Chapter 13 explains. Any change in the size of either of these two liabilities has cash flow impacts that are important to the company's managers as well as its creditors and investors.

Bringing Interest Expense Up to Snuff

Virtually every business has accounts payable and accrued expenses liabilities—which are part and parcel of carrying on its operations. And, most businesses borrow money from a bank or from other sources that lend money to businesses. A note or similar legal instrument is signed when borrowing; hence, the basic liability account is called *notes payable*. Interest is paid on borrowed money, of course, whereas no interest is paid on accounts payable (unless the amount is seriously past due and an interest penalty is added by the creditor). Notes payable always are reported separately and not mixed with non-interest-bearing liabilities.

Interest is a charge per day for the use of borrowed money. Every day money is borrowed increases the amount of interest owed to the lender. The ratio of interest to the amount borrowed is called the interest rate, and always is stated as a percent. Percent means "per hundred." If you borrow $100,000 for one year and pay $8,000 interest, the interest rate is:

$8,000 Interest ÷ $100,000 Borrowed = $8 per $100, or 8%

Interest rates are stated as annual rates, even though the term of a loan is shorter or longer than one year.

Interest is always reported as a separate expense in income statements. It's not the size of interest, but rather the special nature of interest that requires separate disclosure. Interest is a *financial* expense as opposed to operating expenses. Interest depends on how the business is financed, which refers to the company's mix of capital sources. The basic choice is between debt and *equity* (the generic term for all kinds of ownership capital).

You may ask: When is interest paid? It depends. On short-term notes (one year or less) interest is commonly paid in one lump sum at the maturity date of the note, which is the last day of the loan period, at which time the amount borrowed and the accumulated interest are due. On long-term notes (generally any note more than one year) interest is paid semiannually, or possibly monthly or quarterly. In any case, on both short-term and long-term notes there is a lag or delay in paying interest. Nevertheless, interest expense should be recorded for all days the money has been borrowed.

The accumulated amount of unpaid interest expense at the end of the accounting period is calculated and recorded in the *accrued interest expense* liability account—which is just like the accrued operating expenses account, except interest is the expense being recorded. (In external financial reports accrued interest expense may be buried in a broader liability account; it is shown as a separate liability in Exhibit 10.1.) In this example, the amount of unpaid interest expense at year-end is $75,000. (I don't do the actual calculation here.)

It would be proper to include in the interest expense account other types of borrowing costs, such as loan application and processing fees, so-called points charged by lenders, and other incidental costs of borrowing such as legal fees and so on. It's hard to tell from the external financial statements of businesses whether they include these extra charges in the interest expense account or put them in other expense accounts.

EXHIBIT 11.1—INCOME TAX EXPENSE AND INCOME TAX PAYABLE
Dollar Amounts in Thousands

BALANCE SHEET AT END OF YEAR

Assets

Cash	$ 3,265	
Accounts Receivable	5,000	
Inventory	8,450	
Prepaid Expenses	960	
Total Current Assets		$17,675
Property, Plant, and Equipment	$16,500	
Accumulated Depreciation	(4,250)	12,250
Goodwill	$ 7,850	
Accumulated Amortization	(2,275)	5,575
Total Assets		$35,500

INCOME STATEMENT FOR YEAR

Sales Revenue	$52,000
Cost of Goods Sold Expense	33,800
Gross Margin	$18,200
Operating Expenses	12,480
Depreciation Expense	785
Amortization Expense	325
Operating Earnings	$ 4,610
Interest Expense	545
Earnings before Income Tax	$ 4,065
Income Tax Expense	1,423
Net Income	$ 2,642

A relatively small amount of the income tax expense for the year is unpaid at year-end, which is recorded in the Income Tax Payable liability account.

Liabilities and Stockholders' Equity

Accounts Payable—Inventory	$ 2,600	
Accounts Payable—Operating Expenses	720	$ 3,320
Accrued Operating Expenses	$ 1,440	
Accrued Interest Expense	75	1,515
Income Tax Payable		165
Short-Term Notes Payable		3,125
Total Current Liabilities		$ 8,125
Long-Term Notes Payable		4,250
Capital Stock	$ 8,125	
Retained Earnings	15,000	
Total Owners' Equity		23,125
Total Liabilities and Stockholders' Equity		$35,500

11

INCOME TAX EXPENSE AND INCOME TAX PAYABLE

Federal and State Income Taxation
of Business Profit

Please refer to Exhibit 11.1 (page 66), which highlights the connection between *income tax expense* in the income statement and *income tax payable* in the balance sheet. A small part of the company's total income tax expense for the year, which is based on its taxable income for the year, has not been paid at year-end. This remaining balance will be paid over to the tax authorities in the near future. The unpaid portion stays in the company's income tax payable liability account until it is paid.

The business in our example is *incorporated*; the business decided on this form of legal organization (instead of the partnership form or organization as a limited liability company). A corporation, being a separate person in the eyes of the law, has several important advantages. However, profit-motivated business corporations have one serious disadvantage—they are subject to federal and state income tax on their profits.

To be more technical, the business in this example is a regular, or "C" corporation. Under the federal income tax law small or "S" corporations, partnerships, and limited liability companies are "pass-through" tax entities—these entities pay no income tax themselves but instead serve as a conduit. Each year all their taxable income is transferred, or passed through to their owners, who pay individual income tax on their shares of the taxable income. This avoids what is called the "double taxation" of business profit—first in the hands of the business corporation and second in the hands of its stockholders (to the extent that net income is distributed as cash dividends to them).

The first point to keep in mind is that a business corporation must earn *taxable income* to pay income tax. The simplest way to pay no income tax is to have no taxable income, or to have a taxable loss. Of course a business wants to earn profit, but earning a profit comes with the burden of paying income tax on the profit. Once a business enters the profit zone it is subject to income tax.

A second point to keep in mind is that there are many loopholes and options in the federal income tax code—to say nothing about state income tax laws—that reduce or postpone income tax. I suspect you're aware of how complex is our federal income tax law. That's an understatement, if I've ever heard one.

It takes thousands of pages of tax law to define taxable income. Most businesses use income tax professionals to help them determine their taxable income, and to advise them how to minimize their income taxes. In any one year a business might take advantage of several different features of the tax code to minimize its taxable income for the year, or to shift taxable income from one year to other years.

For this example I have to simplify. The business pays a 35% income tax rate on its taxable income. And, the accounting methods used to prepare its income statement are exactly the same methods used to determine its annual taxable income. In this example the company's *earnings before income tax* is $4,065,000 (see Exhibit 11.1). This is also its taxable income for income tax.

With an income tax rate of 35%, its income tax expense for the year is a straightforward calculation:

$$\underset{\text{Taxable Income}}{\$4,065,000} \times \underset{\text{Income Tax Rate}}{35\%} = \underset{\text{Income Tax Expense}}{\$1,423,000}$$

As you see in Exhibit 11.1, the company's income tax expense for the year is exactly this amount.

The federal income tax law requires that a business make installment payments during the year so that 100% of its annual income tax is paid by the end of the year. Actually, a relatively small fraction of the total annual income tax may not be paid by year-end without any penalty (although this can get very complicated).

The company in this example paid the large part of its income tax for the year. At year-end it still owed the Internal Revenue Service $165,000 of its annual income tax. The unpaid portion is recorded in the *income tax payable* account, as you see in Exhibit 11.1.

The federal income tax law changes year to year; Congress is always tinkering, or shall we say "fine-tuning" the tax code. Old loopholes are shut down; new loopholes open up. Tax rates have changed over time. For these reasons the fraction of annual income tax that is unpaid at year-end is hard to predict.

A Short Technical Note: A business may opt to use certain accounting methods to determine its annual taxable income that are more conservative than the accounting methods used to report sales revenue and expenses in its income statement. The objective is to postpone payment of income tax to later years. In this situation generally accepted accounting principles (GAAP) require that the amount of income tax expense in the income statement should be consistent with the amount of earnings before income tax that is reported in the income statement, even though actual taxable income for the year is less. The income tax expense reported in the income statement, therefore, is higher than the amount of income tax actually paid that year. The extra amount of income tax over and above the actual tax paid is recorded in the *deferred income tax* account. This account is reported as a liability in the balance sheet.

EXHIBIT 12.1—NET INCOME INTO RETAINED EARNINGS; EARNINGS PER SHARE (EPS)

Dollar Amounts in Thousands, Except Earnings per Share

INCOME STATEMENT FOR YEAR

Sales Revenue	$52,000
Cost of Goods Sold Expense	33,800
Gross Margin	$18,200
Operating Expenses	12,480
Depreciation Expense	785
Amortization Expense	325
Operating Earnings	$ 4,610
Interest Expense	545
Earnings before Income Tax	$ 4,065
Income Tax Expense	1,423
Net Income	$ 2,642

Earnings per Share $3.30

> Net income for the year is divided by the number of capital stock shares to determine Earnings per Share (EPS):
>
> $2,642,000/800,400 = $3.30

> Bottom-line profit or net income increases the Retained Earnings owners' equity account. (This account is decreased by dividends paid to shareholders.)

BALANCE SHEET AT END OF YEAR

Assets

Cash	$ 3,265	
Accounts Receivable	5,000	
Inventory	8,450	
Prepaid Expenses	960	
Total Current Assets		$17,675
Property, Plant, and Equipment	$16,500	
Accumulated Depreciation	(4,250)	12,250
Goodwill	$ 7,850	
Accumulated Amortization	(2,275)	5,575
Total Assets		**$35,500**

Liabilities and Stockholders' Equity

Accounts Payable—Inventory	$ 2,600	
Accounts Payable—Operating Expenses	720	$ 3,320
Accrued Operating Expenses	$ 1,440	
Accrued Interest Expense	75	1,515
Income Tax Payable		165
Short-Term Notes Payable		3,125
Total Current Liabilities		$ 8,125
Long-Term Notes Payable		4,250
Capital Stock (800,400 shares)	$ 8,125	
Retained Earnings	15,000	
Total Owners' Equity		23,125
Total Liabilities and Stockholders' Equity		**$35,500**

12

NET INCOME AND RETAINED EARNINGS; EARNINGS PER SHARE (EPS)

Net Income into Retained Earnings

Exhibit 12.1 on page 70 highlights the connection from *net income* in the income statement to *retained earnings* in the balance sheet. This chapter explains that earning profit increases the retained earnings account. Also, *earnings per share* (EPS) is explained.

Suppose a business has $10 million total assets and $3 million total liabilities (the total of both non-interest operating liabilities and interest-bearing notes payable), and that its owners have invested $2 million capital in the business. Assets don't just drop down like "manna from heaven." (My old accounting professor was the first person I heard use this phrase, and I've never forgotten it.) The other $5 million of assets must have come from profit it earned but did not distribute—from retained earnings, in other words.

Two separate owners' equity accounts are needed—one for capital invested by the owners and one for retained earnings. When a business distributes money to its owners it must distinguish between returning their capital (which is not taxable to them) versus dividing profit among them (which is taxable). In fact, a business corporation is legally required to keep separate accounts for capital stock and retained earnings.

The income statement reveals that the business earned $2,642,000 profit, or net income for the year. This amount is entered as an increase in retained earnings, which is an owners' equity account. The retained earnings account is so named because annual profit is entered as an increase in the account, and distributions to owners from profit are entered as decreases in the account.

During the year the business paid $750,000 cash dividends from profit to its stockholders. Therefore, its retained earnings increased only $1,892,000 during the year. At the end of the year its retained earnings stands at $15,000,000, which is the cumulative result from all years the company has been in business.

In this example the company obviously has been profitable over the years, given its relatively large retained earnings. Nevertheless, we can't tell from the balance sheet whether the company suffered a loss one or more years in the past, or whether the business regularly pays cash distributions from its annual profits. If a company's losses over the years are larger than its profits, then its retained earnings account would have a *negative* balance, which generally is called *accumulated deficit* or some similar title.

Retained earnings probably is the most misunderstood account in financial statements. Many people, even some experienced business managers, think this account is an asset or, more specifically, cash. Retained earnings is *not* an asset and it certainly is *not* cash. The amount of cash is reported in the cash account in a company's balance sheet ($3,265,000 in this example).

The retained earnings balance, frankly, has little practical significance. Hypothetically, a business could sell all its assets for their book values, pay all its liabilities, return all capital invested in the business to its stockholders, and distribute a "going out of business" cash dividend equal to its retained earnings balance. To stay in business a company can't do this, of course.

Earnings per Share (EPS)

Net income, the bottom line in the income statement, is the profit measure for the business as a whole. Earnings per share (EPS) is the profit measure for each ownership unit, or share in the business.

Suppose in our example that you own 16,008 shares, or exactly 2% of the 800,400 shares of capital stock issued by the business. Several years ago you invested $120,000 in the business, when it was just starting up. You're one of the original stockholders. Your $120,000 capital investment divided by your 16,008 shares means that your cost is about $7.50 per share. Later investors paid more per share.

We can tell this from the balance sheet in Exhibit 12.1. The $8,125,000 balance in the company's capital stock account divided by its 800,400 capital stock shares outstanding works out to an average of a little more than $10 per share. So, the later investors must have paid more than $10 per share, perhaps $20 or more per share.

Since you own only 2% of the total capital stock shares outstanding, you are a passive, outside investor in the business. You do not participate actively in managing the company. Of course you're entitled to 2% of any cash dividends paid from profit, and you control 2% of the votes on matters that have to be put to a vote of stockholders.

As a stockholder you are provided a copy of the company's annual (and quarterly) financial reports. Needless to say, you're very interested in the company's profit performance. You could take the view that 2% of annual net income "belongs" to you, which is a $52,840 slice of the company's $2,642,000 net income. This is your cut of the net income pie.

Or, you could look at earnings per share (EPS), which is net income divided by the number of capital stock shares. In this example EPS for the year just ended is:

$$\frac{\$2,642,000 \text{ Net Income}}{800,400 \text{ Capital Stock Shares}} = \$3.30 \text{ EPS}$$

Generally accepted accounting principles (GAAP) distinguish between nonpublic companies, whose capital stock shares are not traded in any established marketplace, and public companies, whose shares are traded on the New York Stock Exchange or through another national stock market such as Nasdaq. Only public companies have to report EPS at the bottom of their income statements. Nonpublic companies can report EPS if they want to, though I don't think many do.

EPS is compared with the market price of the stock shares. The ratio of current market value to EPS (called the price/earnings ratio) is discussed in Chapter 22. There are no active markets for stock shares of nonpublic or privately owned business corporations. Nevertheless, the stockholders in nonpublic businesses can use EPS to make an estimate of the value of their stock shares.

For example, suppose I offered to buy 1,000 of your shares. You might offer to sell them at 15 times the $3.30 EPS, or $49.50 per share. Of course, I might not be willing to pay this price, but you could ask. There is the need to put a current value on stock shares for estate tax purposes when someone dies. EPS is one basis for putting an estimated value on capital stock shares. EPS is discussed further in Chapter 22.

EXHIBIT 13.1—CASH FLOW FROM PROFIT (OPERATING ACTIVITIES) FOR YEAR
Dollar Amounts in Thousands

BALANCE SHEET	End of Year	Start of Year	Change		STATEMENT OF CASH FLOWS FOR YEAR		
Assets					Net Income—See Income Statement	$ 2,642	
Cash	$ 3,265	$ 3,735	$ (470)		Accounts Receivable Increase	(320)	
Accounts Receivable	5,000	4,680	320		Inventory Increase	(935)	
Inventory	8,450	7,515	935		Prepaid Expenses Increase	(275)	
Prepaid Expenses	960	685	275		Depreciation Expense	785	
Property, Plant, and Equipment	16,500	13,450	3,050		Amortization Expenses	325	
Accumulated Depreciation	(4,250)	(3,465)	(785)		Accounts Payable Increase	645	
Goodwill	7,850	6,950	900		Accrued Expenses Increase	480	
Accumulated Amortization	(2,275)	(1,950)	(325)		Income Tax Payable Increase	83	
Total Assets	$35,500	$31,600			**Cash Flow from Operating Activities**		$ 3,430
					Purchases of Property, Plant, and Equipment	$(3,050)	
Liabilities and Stockholders' Equity					Purchase of Goodwill	(900)	
Accounts Payable	$ 3,320	$ 2,675	$ 645		**Cash Flow from Investing Activities**		$(3,950)
Accrued Expenses	1,515	1,035	480				
Income Tax Payable	165	82	83				
Short-Term Notes Payable	3,125	3,000	125		Increase in Short-Term Notes Payable	$ 125	
Long-Term Notes Payable	4,250	3,750	500		Increase in Long-Term Notes Payable	500	
Capital Stock	8,125	7,950	175		Issue of Additional Capital Stock Shares	175	
Retained Earnings	15,000	13,108	1,892		Cash Dividends Paid Shareholders	(750)	
Total Liabilities and Stockholders' Equity	$35,500	$31,600			**Cash Flow from Financing Activities**		$ 50
					Decrease in Cash during Year		$ (470)

13

CASH FLOW FROM PROFIT AND LOSS

Profit and Cash Flow from Profit: Not Identical Twins!

At this point we shift gears. Chapters 4 through 12 (except for Chapter 6) walk down the income statement. Each chapter explains how sales revenue or an expense is connected with its corresponding operating asset or liability. In short, sales revenue and expenses cause changes in assets and liabilities. You can't understand the balance sheet too well without understanding how sales revenue and expenses drive many of the assets and liabilities in the balance sheet.

This chapter is the first of two that explain the *statement of cash flows*, which is the third primary financial statement reported by businesses in addition to the income statement and balance sheet (also called the statement of financial condition). Exhibit 13.1 on page 76 presents the official format for the cash flow statement of the business we have discussed since Chapter 1. Please take a moment to read down this statement. I'll make you a wager here. I bet you understand the second and third sections of the statement (investing activities and financing activities) much better than the first section (operating activities).

Exhibit 13.1 shows the comparative balance sheet of the company and includes a column for changes in assets, liabilities, and owners' equities. These increases and decreases directly tie in with the statement of cash flows. This chapter focuses on the first section of the cash flow statement, which presents cash flow from the company's profit-making operations during the year.

The main question on everyone's mind is why profit doesn't equal cash flow. In this example the company earned $2,642,000 net income. Why didn't profit (net income) generate the same amount of cash flow? The purpose of the first section in the cash flow statement is to answer this question.

The last line in this section is labeled "Cash Flow from Operating Activities," as you see in Exhibit 13.1. Frankly, this is not the best name in the world. I prefer to call it *cash flow from profit*. The term "operating activities" is accounting jargon for sales revenue and expenses, which are the profit-making activities or operations of a business. Most of the time I'll refer to this line as cash flow from profit, which is shorter and more descriptive, I think. In any case, from the cash flow statement we see that the company generated $3,430,000 cash flow from profit compared with the considerably smaller $2,642,000 net income for the year.

Business managers have a double duty—first to earn profit, and second to convert the profit into cash as soon as possible. Waiting too long to turn profit into cash reduces its value because of the time value of money. Business managers should be clear on the difference between profit reported in the income statement and the amount of cash flow from profit during the year. Creditors and investors also should pay attention to cash flow from profit and management's ability to control this very important number.

To get from net income to its cash flow result we have to make adjustments along the way. Each is caused by a change during the year in one of the company's operating assets and liabilities (i.e., the assets and liabilities directly involved in sales revenue and expenses). We shall look at these adjustments in the order shown in the company's statement of cash flows (data is from in Exhibit 13.1, page 76).

Eight Changes in Operating Assets and Liabilities That Determine Cash Flow from Profit for Year

1. *Accounts Receivable:* At year-end the company had $5,000,000 uncollected sales revenue, which is the ending balance of its accounts receivable. The $5,000,000 is included in sales revenue for determining profit. But the company did not receive this amount of cash from customers. The $5,000,000 went into accounts receivable instead of cash. On the other hand, the company collected its $4,680,000 beginning balance of accounts receivable. The $4,680,000 collected minus $5,000,000 not collected has a $320,000 negative impact on cash flow. See the first adjustment in the cash flow statement (Exhibit 13.1, page 76). If short, an increase in accounts receivable hurts cash flow from profit.

2. *Inventory:* Notice the rather large increase in the company's inventory during the year. This may or may not have been a smart business decision. Perhaps the business

needed a larger inventory to meet higher sales demand; maybe not. In any case, the $935,000 inventory increase has a negative impact on cash flow from profit. The quickest way to explain this is as follows. The company paid for all the products sold during the year, which is reported in cost of goods sold expense for determining profit. Plus, it spent an additional $935,000 to build up its inventory. It's almost as if the company had to write $935,000 of checks to enlarge its inventory. See the second adjustment in the cash flow statement. In short, an increase in inventory hurts cash flow from profit.

So far, cash flow is down $1,255,000—the $320,000 negative adjustment for accounts receivable plus the $935,000 negative adjustment for inventory. The next item also hurts cash flow from profit.

3. *Prepaid Expenses:* During the year the company paid $960,000 for certain operating costs that will benefit next year, and therefore were *not* charged to operating expenses in the year. See the ending balance in the company's prepaid expenses account. The company paid $960,000 on top of its operating expenses for the year. But the company had $685,000 of prepaid expenses at the start of the year; these costs were paid last year and then charged to operating expenses in the year just ended. Taking into account both the beginning and ending balances in prepaid expenses, the company experiences only $275,000 drain on cash during the year. The $685,000 not paid minus $960,000 paid has a $275,000 negative impact on cash flow. See the third adjustment in the cash flow statement.

4. **Depreciation:** During the year the company recorded $785,000 depreciation expense, *not* by writing a check for this amount but by writing down the cost of its property, plant, and equipment. This write-down is recorded as an increase in the accumulated depreciation account, which is the contra or offset account deducted from the property, plant, and equipment asset account. These long-term operating assets are partially written down each year to record the wear and tear on the resources every year of use. The company paid cash for the assets when it bought these long-term resources. The company does not have to pay for them a second time when it uses them. In short, depreciation expense is not a cash outlay in the year recorded and therefore is a positive adjustment to determine cash flow from profit. See the fourth adjustment in the cash flow statement.

The depreciation "add back" to net income can be explained another way. For the sake of argument here, assume all sales revenue was collected in cash during the year. Part of this cash inflow from customers pays the company for the use of its long-term operating assets during the year. In a sense the business "sells" a fraction of its fixed assets to its customers each year. In setting its sales prices a business includes depreciation as a cost of doing business. So, each year a business recovers part of the capital invested in its fixed assets in the cash flow from sales revenue. In short, the company in this example recaptured or recouped $785,000 of the investment in its property, plant, and equipment assets, which is a significant source of cash flow.

5. **Amortization:** From the cash flow viewpoint this expense is virtually the same as depreciation expense. The $325,000 amortization expense for the year is recorded by decreasing the company's goodwill asset account (i.e., by increasing the accumulated amortization account that is deducted from the goodwill asset account). In brief, amortization is an asset write-down type expense, just like depreciation. There was no cash outlay during the year for the expense. The business expended cash when it paid for the goodwill that it purchased sometime in prior years. Therefore, the $325,000 amortization amount is added back to net income for determining cash flow from operating activities, or profit—see Exhibit 13.1 again.

6. **Accounts Payable:** The ending balances in the company's accounts payable reveal that manufacturing costs and operating expenses were not fully paid during the year. The ending balances in this liability relieved the company of making cash payments in the amount of $3,320,000 (again see Exhibit 13.1). Not paying these costs avoids cash outflow, of course. But consider the other side of the coin. The company started the year with $2,675,000 accounts payable. These liabilities were paid during the year. The $3,320,000 not paid minus $2,675,000 paid has a net $645,000 positive impact on cash flow. See the sixth adjustment in the cash flow statement.

7. **Accrued Expenses:** This liability works virtually the same as accounts payable. The company did not pay $1,515,000 of its expenses during the year, which is the balance in this liability at the end of the year. But the company did pay the $1,035,000 beginning amounts of this liability. The $1,515,000 not paid minus $1,035,000 paid has a net $480,000 positive impact on cash flow. See the seventh adjustment in the cash flow statement.

8. Income Tax Payable: At the start of the year the business owed the tax authorities $82,000 on taxable income from the previous year. This amount was paid early in the year. At the end of the year the business owed $165,000 of its income tax expense for the year; this amount was not paid. The net effect is that the company paid $83,000 less to the government than its income tax expense for the year. See the positive adjustment for the increase in income tax payable in the cash flow statement.

Summing up the cash flow adjustments to net income:

• Increases in operating assets cause decreases in cash flow from profit; and decreases in operating assets result in increases in cash flow from profit. There is a *reverse effect* on cash flow, in other words.

• Increases in operating liabilities help cash flow from profit; and decreases in operating liabilities result in decreases in cash flow from profit. There is a *same way effect* on cash flow, in other words.

See in Exhibit 13.1 that the combined net effect of the eight adjustments is that cash flow from profit is $3,430,000, which is $788,000 more than profit for the year. This "extra" cash flow is due to the changes in the company's operating assets and liabilities. In summary, business realized $3,430,000 cash flow from its operating activities during the year. This source of cash flow is vital to every business.

One last point: The accounting profession's rule-making body, the Financial Accounting Standards Board (FASB), has expressed a preference regarding reporting cash flow from operating activities. The format you see in Exhibit 13.1 is called the *indirect method*, which uses the changes in operating assets and liabilities to adjust net income. Instead, the FASB prefers the *direct method* for this section of the statement of cash flows.

Exhibit 13.2 on page 82 shows the *direct* method format for reporting cash flows from operating activities for our business example. This direct format is supplemented with a schedule that reports changes in operating assets and liabilities, pretty much the same way as the changes are presented by the indirect method (Exhibit 13.1). Both formats report the same flow from operating activities, of course. Despite the FASB's clear preference for the direct method, the large majority of businesses use the indirect method in their external financial reports (which the FASB permits).

Note: You might compare Exhibit 13.2 here with Exhibit 3.2 on page 22 in Chapter 3, which shows how each of the cash flows reported by the direct method are determined, based on the changes in the company's operating assets and liabilities at the start of the period and the end of the period.

What Does "Cash Flow" Mean?

More and more in the business and financial press you see "cash flow" mentioned in articles and stories. It may surprise you that there is no standardized definition of cash flow. At a recent party

EXHIBIT 13.2—DIRECT METHOD FORMAT FOR REPORTING CASH FLOW FROM OPERATING ACTIVITIES IN THE STATEMENT OF CASH FLOWS
Dollar Amounts in Thousands

Sales Revenue	$51,680
Cost of Goods Sold Expense	(34,435)
Operating Expenses	(11,955)
Interest Expense	(520)
Income Tax Expense	(1,340)
Cash Flow from Operating Activities	$ 3,430

items (dollar amounts in thousands; data from Exhibits 12.1 and 13.1):

Calculation of EBITDA

Net income	$2,642
+ Interest	545
+ Income tax	1,423
+ Depreciation	785
+ Amortization	325
= EBITDA	$5,720

a colleague asked me what is meant by the term "cash flow." I had to tell him that it could refer to a number of different things. When I read articles in the *Wall Street Journal* that use the term "cash flow" I'm not sure what the reporter means by the term. Reporters usually don't offer definitions of this term in their articles. But when they do they don't necessarily mean the line in the cash flow statement that we've been analyzing (i.e., cash flow from operating activities).

The main contender to cash flow from operating activities is earnings before interest, (income) tax, depreciation, and amortization (EBITDA). Starting with net income for our example, EBITDA is determined by adding back those

EBITDA is a measure of cash flow from *operating* earnings—cash flow the business generated from its nuts-and-bolts operations before the financial expense of interest is considered and before the government's share for income tax is taken into account. EBITDA should be used very carefully and with a crystal-clear understanding that this cash flow measure is not the bottom-line cash flow from operating activities, because cash flows for interest and income tax expenses are not taken into account.

A much more crude way to measure cash flow from profit is simply to start with net income (bottom-line profit) and add back depreciation and amortization expenses because these two expenses do not require cash outlays during the period. Keep in mind that changes in accounts receivable, inventory, prepaid expenses, accounts payable, accrued expenses payable, and income tax payable are ignored by this method. If all these changes in operating assets and liabilities are relatively minor, then simply adding back depreciation and amortization to net income is acceptable. But typically all these changes are not minor and therefore they should not be ignored.

One final caution: The notion of cash flow is like an elixir, which suggests more than it is. When a business's profit is lackluster or it reports a loss the CEO is very likely to shift attention to cash flow (assuming its cash flow is positive). But cash flow is not a substitute for profit. The oldest trick in the book is to divert attention from bad news to whatever good news you can find. Simply put, profit generates cash flow; cash flow does not generate profit.

EXHIBIT 14.1—CASH FLOWS FROM INVESTING AND FINANCING ACTIVITIES FOR YEAR
Dollar Amounts in Thousands

BALANCE SHEET	End of Year	Start of Year	Change
Assets			
Cash	$ 3,265	$ 3,735	$ (470)
Accounts Receivable	5,000	4,680	320
Inventory	8,450	7,515	935
Prepaid Expenses	960	685	275
Property, Plant, and Equipment	16,500	13,450	3,050
Accumulated Depreciation	(4,250)	(3,465)	(785)
Goodwill	7,850	6,950	900
Accumulated Amortization	(2,275)	(1,950)	(325)
Total Assets	$35,500	$31,600	
Liabilities and Stockholders' Equity			
Accounts Payable	$ 3,320	$ 2,675	$ 645
Accrued Expenses	1,515	1,035	480
Income Tax Payable	165	82	83
Short-Term Notes Payable	3,125	3,000	125
Long-Term Notes Payable	4,250	3,750	500
Capital Stock	8,125	7,950	175
Retained Earnings	15,000	13,108	1,892
Total Liabilities and Stockholders' Equity	$35,500	$31,600	

STATEMENT OF CASH FLOWS FOR YEAR		
New Income	$ 2,642	
Accounts Receivable Increase	(320)	
Inventory Increase	(935)	
Prepaid Expenses Increase	(275)	
Depreciation Expense	785	
Amortization Expenses	325	
Accounts Payable Increase	645	
Accrued Expenses Increase	480	
Income Tax Payable Increase	83	
Cash Flow from Operating Activities		$ 3,430
Purchases of Property, Plant, and Equipment	$(3,050)	
Purchase of Goodwill	(900)	
Cash Flow from Investing Activities		$(3,950)
Increase in Short-Term Notes Payable	$ 125	
Increase in Long-Term Notes Payable	500	
Issue of Additional Capital Stock Shares	175	
Cash Dividends Paid Shareholders	(750)	
Cash Flow from Financing Activities		$ 50
Decrease in Cash during Year		$ (470)

14

CASH FLOWS FROM INVESTING AND FINANCING ACTIVITIES

Nonprofit Sources of Cash; Uses of Cash

Profit is a vital source of cash inflow to every business. Profit is *internal* cash flow—money generated by the business itself without going outside the company to external sources of capital. Chapter 13 explains that the company's profit generated $3,430,000 cash flow during the year just ended. Profit provided more than three million dollars of money for the business, and this isn't chicken feed.

The obvious question is: What did the business do with its cash flow from profit? The remainder of the cash flow statement provides the answer to this question; it also reports other sources of cash that were tapped by the business during the year that provided additional capital to the business.

The company had $3,430,000 cash available during the year. What *could* it do with this money? (We'll look at what it actually did in just a moment.) One option is simply to increase its cash balance—just let the money pile up in the company's checking account. This is not a very productive use of the cash, unless the business were on the ragged edge and desperately needed more cash to work with. Or, the business could pay off some of its debt. Or, the company could use some of the money to pay cash dividends to its stockholders.

In fact, the business did pay $750,000 cash dividends to its stockholders during the year. The total amount of cash dividends to shareholders is one of the key items reported in the statement of cash flows—see Exhibit 14.1 on page 84. After cash dividends, the company had $2,680,000 cash flow remaining from operating activities ($3,430,000 cash flow from operating activities less

$750,000 cash dividends = $2,680,000). So you may ask: What did the business do with this cash?

To modernize and expand its production and sales capacity, the business invested $3,950,000 in new long-term (fixed) operating assets during the year (refer to Exhibit 14.1 again for this information). These cash outlays are called *capital expenditures*, to emphasize the long-term nature of investing capital in these assets. You may have noticed that the total amount of capital expenditures was considerably more than the amount of cash flow from profit net of cash dividends ($3,950,000 capital expenditures less $2,680,000 cash flow from profit net of cash dividends = $1,270,000 shortfall). This money had to come from somewhere.

Basically the business had three sources of cash to cover the $1,270,000 shortfall: (1) borrow more money on short-term and long-term debt; (2) secure additional capital from shareowners by issuing new capital stock; and (3) use up some of its cash balance. The business did some of all three (amounts from Exhibit 14.1):

Other Sources of Cash and Decrease in Cash Balance Used to Finance Capital Expenditures during Year

Short-term debt increase	$ 125,000
Long-term debt increase	500,000
Issue of new capital stock shares	175,000
Decrease in cash balance	470,000
Total	$1,270,000

When a business is growing from year to year its cash flow from profit net of cash dividends does not provide all the cash it needs for its capital expenditures. Therefore, the business has to expand its debt and equity capital, which the business did in our example.

Managers and other financial report readers keep a close watch on capital expenditures. These cash outlays are a "bet on the future" by the company. The business is saying, in effect, that it needs the new fixed assets to maintain or improve its competitive position, or to expand its facilities for future growth. These are some of the most critical decisions made by management.

Making such investments is always risky. Who knows what will happen in the future? But, on the other hand, not making such investments may sign the death warrant of a business; by not making such investments the company may fall behind its competition and lose market share that would be impossible to regain. Then again, being overinvested and having excess capacity can be an albatross around the neck of the business.

In any case, the business laid out $3,950,000 during the year for new assets (see Exhibit 14.1 again). In doing so the business had to make key financing decisions—where to get the money for the asset purchases. As already mentioned, the business decided it could allow its working cash balance to drop by $470,000. The company's ending cash balance is $3,265,000, which relative to its $52,000,000 annual sales revenue equals a little more than three weeks of sales revenue.

I should point out that there are no general standards or guidelines regarding how large a company's working cash balance should be. The company's cash balance in this example would be viewed as adequate by most business managers, I think. Just how much cash cushion does a business need as a safety reserve to protect against unfavorable developments?

What if the economy takes a nosedive, or what if the company has a serious falloff in sales? What if some of its accounts receivable are not collected on time? What if the company is not able to sell its inventory soon enough to start the cash flow cycle in motion? What if it doesn't have enough money to pay its employees on time? There are no easy answers to the many cash balance issues.

The business could have forgone cash dividends in order to keep its working cash balance at a higher level. Probably, its stockholders want a cash dividend on their investments in the business, and the board of directors was under pressure to deliver cash dividends. In any case, the business did pay $750,000 cash dividends, which are reported in the financing activities section in the cash flow statement (Exhibit 14.1).

Should cash dividends be reported as a direct deduction under cash flow from operating activities (profit), to show more explicitly how much cash flow was available from profit after cash dividends? This would draw attention to a key cash flow number of the business. I suspect that most companies do not want to call attention to this number. The Fiinancial Accounting Standards Board (FASB) decided that dividends should be reported in the financing activities section of the cash flow statement. I favor more options on this matter.

In summary, the cash flow statement deserves as much attention and scrutiny as the income statement and balance sheet. Though not too likely, a company making profit could be headed for liquidity problems (having too little ready cash) or solvency problems (not being able to pay liabilities on time). Profit does not guarantee liquidity and solvency. The cash flow statement should be read carefully to see if there are any danger signs or red flags.

One Last Point: Having just encouraged you to read this financial statement, I should mention that cash flow statements as reported by most public corporations are cluttered with a lot of detail—far too much detail, in my opinion. One could get the impression that companies are deliberately making their cash flow statements hard to read, though this view may be too cynical.

Anyway, you should look mainly at the big-ticket items and skip many of the smaller details. Income statements reported by most public corporations, in sharp contrast, have fewer lines of information than cash flow statements and are generally much easier to read and understand. This is an odd state of affairs indeed.

15

GROWTH, DECLINE, AND CASH FLOW

Setting the Stage for Cash Flow

Chapter 13 explains how changes in a company's operating assets and operating liabilities help or hurt cash flow from profit. To review briefly, there are three major pieces to the cash flow puzzle—depreciation and amortization, operating assets, and operating liabilities:

- **Depreciation and Amortization:** During the year a business converts part of the capital invested in its long-term tangible and intangible assets into cash. Sales revenue reimburses a business for expenses the company incurs in making the sales. (Profit is the margin by which sales revenue exceeds expenses.) One expense is depreciation of the company's fixed assets. Another is amortization of the company's intangible assets (in this example goodwill). A part of the sales revenue collected during the year pays for the use of the company's long-term operating assets during the year. In a real sense customers pay the business "rent" on these assets. For example, when you pay for a meal in a restaurant part of your bill compensates the business for your use of its kitchen equipment, tables, chairs, and so forth.

- **Operating Assets:** Net income plus depreciation and amortization is not the whole story for cash flow from profit. Changes in a company's operating assets (accounts receivable, inventory, and prepaid expenses) also affect cash flow from profit. Increases in these assets put a damper on cash flow. Some of the cash inflow from sales revenue is used for these increases in operating assets. Decreases in operating assets improve cash flow from profit; the business, in effect, liquidates part of its investments in these assets.

- **Operating Liabilities:** Increases in operating liabilities (accounts payable, accrued expenses, and income tax payable) help cash flow from profit during the year. The business avoids cash outlay to the extent of the increases. In other words, part of total expenses for the year are not paid but instead are recorded by increases in these liabilities. Decreases in operating liabilities have the opposite effect; more cash is paid out than the amount of expenses for the year.

A business records depreciation expense every year on its property, plant, and equipment (except land). Depreciation is an "add back" to net income every year to determine cash flow from profit. This means that every year a business recovers some of the cost invested in its fixed assets from sales revenue cash inflow. The amount of depreciation expense varies year to year, but every year a business recoups a fraction of its investment in fixed assets.

Depreciation cash inflow can be used to replace old fixed assets that have reached the ends of their useful lives. However, the amount of depreciation recapture may not be enough to provide all the cash needed for new fixed assets. Depreciation based on original cost cannot be expected to provide enough cash flow to replace the assets at higher current costs, much less to expand the fixed assets of a business.

Cash Flow in the Steady-State Case

Let's look ahead to next year for the business example I've used throughout the book. In broad terms the company's sales revenue next year will hold steady, grow, or decline. These are the three scenarios for next year. The scenarios have remarkably different impacts on cash flow from operating activities (i.e., cash flow from profit).

We start with the steady state (i.e., the no growth/no decline scenario) for the business example. Exhibit 15.1 on this page presents the first section of the company's cash flow statement next year for this hypothetical situation. The purpose is to demonstrate what happens to cash flow from profit next year if sales revenue and expenses next year are a carbon copy of the year just ended.

Exhibit 15.1 rests on one key premise—that the company's operating assets and liabilities would hold steady next year. For example, if the company's sales revenue next year is the same, then there is no reason for its accounts receivable to change. Likewise, if cost of goods sold expense remains the same next year, there is no reason for the company's inventory to increase or decrease. And likewise for prepaid expenses, accounts payable, accrued expenses, and income tax payable. Therefore, Exhibit 15.1 shows zero changes for all operating assets and liabilities. The only cash flow adjustments to net income, consequently, are the add backs for depreciation and amortization expenses.

Now, a company's sales revenue and expenses next year will almost certainly change, at least a little bit. The purpose here,

EXHIBIT 15.1—CASH FLOW FROM PROFIT (OPERATING ACTIVITIES) IN STEADY-STATE SCENARIO
Dollar Amounts in Thousands

Net Income	$2,642
Accounts Receivable Change	0
Inventory Change	0
Prepaid Expenses Change	0
Depreciation Expense	795
Amortization Expense	325
Accounts Payable Change	0
Accrued Expenses Change	0
Income Tax Payable Change	0
Cash Flow from Operating Activities	$3,762

however, is to provide a useful point of departure before moving onto the growth and decline scenarios. Exhibit 15.1 highlights two key points. The first is the unique nature of depreciation and amortization. Exhibit 15.1 makes these two expenses stick out like a sore thumb. This is the only situation in which cash flow from profit equals net income plus depreciation and amortization.

The second point concerns those zeros in Exhibit 15.1, representing no changes in the company's operating assets and liabilities. Zero changes happen only if the company keeps its *operating ratios* constant between its income statement accounts and their corresponding balance sheet accounts. For instance, in this example the company's accounts receivable equals 5 weeks of annual sales revenue, its inventory equals 13 weeks of annual cost of goods sold expense, and so on. These ratios may change from one year to the next, but not in this scenario.

For instance, even in a steady-state situation the business may allow its average accounts receivable collection period to drift up to 6 weeks of annual sales, in which case its accounts receivable would increase. This increase would cause a negative cash flow adjustment. So, even if sales revenue and expenses remain constant next year, a company's operating assets and liabilities may change because the average credit period extended to its customers may change, its average inventory holding period may change, its average credit period of accounts payable may change, and so on.

Cash flow from profit in the steady-state scenario is like milking a cow that gives a dependable supply of cash flow every period equal to depreciation and amortization plus net income. Growth and decline situations are entirely different—as we shall see in the next two sections.

Growth "Penalty" on Cash Flow from Profit

Growth is the central strategy of most businesses. The purpose of growth, of course, is to increase profit and shareholders' wealth. Without good management, however, expenses may grow faster than sales revenue, and profit may actually decrease. In tough times just holding its own may be the best a business can do.

Exhibit 15.2 on page 95 presents a growth scenario for the business for next year. The exhibit focuses on *changes* in the company's income statement, balance sheet, and cash flow statement. The company is budgeting significant growth in sales revenue and profit for next year, and wants to know how this growth will impact the company's cash flow from profit next year.

On the left side in Exhibit 15.2 is the company's income statement for the year just ended. Budgeted changes for next year are entered in the second column. (We do not go into how the company arrived at these changes; we trust that the company's managers have done realistic forecasting and have set achievable goals for next year.)

Exhibit 15.2 starts with the changes in sales revenue and expenses, then moves across to changes in operating assets and liabilities that are caused by the changes in sales revenue and expenses, and then moves over to the cash flow statement where the changes in the operating assets and liabilities are entered as adjustments to net income.

The changes in operating assets and liabilities assume that the company's operating ratios remain the same. For instance, notice that cost of goods sold expense is budgeted to increase $4,225,000 next year. The company's inventory is 13 weeks of annual cost of goods sold; so, the increase in cost of goods sold expense causes the amount invested in inventory to increase accordingly ($4,225,000 increase in cost of goods sold expense × 13/52 operating ratio = $1,056,000 increase in inventory). All other operating ratios are held constant in the growth scenario shown in Exhibit 15.2 as well. Also notice that depreciation expense is budgeted to increase $95,000 next year, because the company plans on buying new fixed assets. So, depreciation is $880,000 next year.

Profit is budgeted to increase $350,000 next year, to $2,992,000. This is good, of course. But, please do not assume that cash flow from profit next year will increase $350,000, which would be $3,430,000 cash flow for the year just ended plus $350,000 or $3,780,000 cash flow next year. The business will not have this much cash flow from profit, not by a long shot.

Exhibit 15.2 reveals that cash flow from profit next year will be only $3,056,000. This lower amount of cash flow is due to rather large "hits" on cash flow caused by the increases in accounts receivable and inventory next year that are needed to support the higher level of sales and expenses. These sizable negative adjustments to cash flow are offset to some extent by increases in operating liabilities. But the company ends up with

EXHIBIT 15.2—CASH FLOW FROM PROFIT (OPERATING ACTIVITIES) IN GROWTH SCENARIO
Dollar Amounts in Thousands

INCOME STATEMENT

	Year Just Ended	Budgeted Changes Next Year
Sales Revenue	$52,000	$6,500
Cost of Goods Sold	33,800	4,225
Gross Margin	$18,200	$2,275
Operating Expenses	12,480	1,560
Depreciation Expense	785	95
Amortization Expense	325	45
Operating Earnings	$ 4,610	$ 575
Interest Expense	545	35
Earnings before Tax	$ 4,065	$ 540
Income Tax Expense	1,423	190
Net Income	$ 2,642	$ 350
Budgeted Net Income for Next Year		$2,992

BALANCE SHEET

	Budgeted Changes Next Year
Assets	
Cash	$3,056
Accounts Receivable	625
Inventory	1,056
Prepaid Expenses	120
Accumulated Depreciation	(880)
Accumulated Amortization	(370)
Total	$3,607
Liabilities and Owners' Equity	
Accounts Payable	$ 415
Accrued Expenses	185
Income Tax Payable	15
Retained Earnings	2,992
Total	$3,607

Budgeted Cash Flow from Operating Activities Next Year

Net Income	$2,992
Accounts Receivable Increase	(625)
Inventory Increase	(1,056)
Prepaid Expenses Increase	(120)
Depreciation Expense	880
Amortization Expense	370
Accounts Payable Increase	415
Accrued Expenses Increase	185
Income Tax Payable Increase	15
Income Tax Payable Increase	$3,056

Note: During the coming year the business would have investing and financing transactions that are not reflected in this exhibit.

over $3 million cash flow from net income, which is a smidgen more than next year's budgeted profit.

In short, there's no such thing as a free lunch for growth when it comes to cash flow. Growth should be good for profit next year, but almost always puts a crimp in cash flow next year. In other words, growth does not produce instant cash flow equal to the increase in profit. Compare Exhibit 15.2, which shows cash flow from profit for the growth scenario, with Exhibit 15.1, which shows cash flow from profit in the steady-state scenario. Cash flow is much higher in the steady-state case. Profit is lower in the steady-state case, but cash flow is higher.

A business could speed up cash flow from profit next year if it were able to improve its operating ratios, such as holding less inventory. But, generally speaking, improving operating ratios is very difficult in a period of growth. If anything, a business may be under pressure and allow its operating ratios to slip a little. For example, the company may offer customers more liberal credit terms to stimulate sales, which would extend the average accounts receivable credit period. Or, the business may increase the size and mix of its inventory to improve delivery times to customers and to provide better selection.

Exhibit 15.2 does not show the company's other sources of cash flow or how it plans to use available cash during the coming year. In other words, the financing and investing sections of the cash flow statement are not presented. We don't see, for instance, how much the business is planning to spend on capital expenditures next year, or how much the company plans to distribute in cash dividends to its stockholders next year. Exhibit 15.2 presents the all-important cash flow from profit, which is the essential starting point for cash flow planning next year.

Cash Flow "Reward" from Decline

The old saying "what goes up can come down" certainly applies to sales revenue and the financial fortunes of a business. Few businesses can keep growing forever, without eventually slowing down or reversing direction. Of course there are the examples of remarkable long-run sustained growth, such as Wal-Mart and Microsoft. But even stalwarts such as McDonald's have leveled off or declined. Some industries are cyclical by nature; their sales revenue goes up and down like a roller coaster over the cycle.

Profit performance almost always suffers in a decline. It's very difficult for a business to respond to a sharp falloff in sales by cutting its expenses immediately. For one thing, most businesses are saddled with fixed costs that stay the same even when sales volume declines. A business has to do major surgery to reduce its fixed costs. Chapter 23 explains the impact of fixed costs on profit behavior. This present chapter focuses on the consequences of decline on cash flow from profit.

Exhibit 15.3 on page 98 presents a decline scenario for the business, which we might call the "evil twin" of the growth scenario shown in Exhibit 15.2. In comparing the two exhibits, notice first that sales revenue goes down $6,500,000 in this scenario, which is a big drop. Cost of goods sold expense drops $4,225,000, which is consistent with the drop in sales revenue. However, the company's other expenses do not decrease proportionally with sales revenue, mainly because of the fixed-cost components in the expenses. (Chapter 23 goes into this topic.)

The bottom line, as they say, is that net income would fall $450,000, about one-sixth of last year's profit. This is bad news, of course. The good news is that cash flow from profit would be higher, much higher. Net income would drop to $2,192,000, but cash flow from profit would be over $4 million! You may find this rather surprising.

The scenario presented in Exhibit 15.3 assumes that the company does not change any of its operating ratios. For example, the ratio of accounts receivable to annual sales revenue remains at 5 weeks. Since sales revenue drops $6,500,000, accounts receivable drops $625,000 ($6,500,000 decrease in sales revenue × 5/52 weeks = $625,000 decrease in accounts receivable). Notice in Exhibit 15.3 that every operating asset and liability drops—including income tax payable because the business is budgeting a decrease in taxable income next year.

Notice the large positive adjustments in Exhibit 15.3 due to changes in accounts receivable and inventory. In short, the business would realize a substantial cash flow from profit and would have to decide what to do with the cash.

The company could pay off a substantial part of its debt (interest-bearing liabilities) or possibly retire some of its capital stock shares. If the business predicts that the decline will be permanent, it will not need as much capital from debt and equity sources. At the lower level of sales the company needs lower asset levels, which means it needs less capital.

EXHIBIT 15.3—CASH FLOW FROM PROFIT (OPERATING ACTIVITIES) IN DECLINE SCENARIO

Dollar Amounts in Thousands

INCOME STATEMENT

	Year Just Ended	Budgeted Changes Next Year
Sales Revenue	$52,000	$(6,500)
Cost of Goods Sold	33,800	(4,225)
Gross Margin	$18,200	$(2,275)
Operating Expenses	12,480	(1,560)
Depreciation Expense	785	0
Amortization Expense	325	0
Operating Earnings	$ 4,610	$ (715)
Interest Expense	545	(25)
Earnings before Tax	$ 4,065	$ (690)
Income Tax Expense	1,423	(240)
Net Income	$ 2,642	$ (450)
Budgeted Net Income for Next Year		$ 2,192

BALANCE SHEET

	Budgeted Changes Next Year
Assets	
Cash	$4,468
Accounts Receivable	(625)
Inventory	(1,056)
Prepaid Expenses	(120)
Accumulated Depreciation	(785)
Accumulated Amortization	(325)
Total	$1,557
Liabilities and Owners' Equity	
Accounts Payable	$ (415)
Accrued Expenses	(175)
Income Tax Payable	(45)
Retained Earnings	2,192
Total	$1,557

Budgeted Cash Flow from Operating Activities Next Year

Net Income	$2,192
Accounts Receivable Decrease	625
Inventory Decrease	1,056
Prepaid Expenses Decrease	120
Depreciation Expense	785
Amortization Expense	325
Accounts Payable Decrease	(415)
Accrued Expenses Decrease	(175)
Income Tax Payable Decrease	(45)
	$4,468

Note: During the coming year the business would have investing and financing transactions that are not reflected in this exhibit.

The broader challenge facing the business concerns developing a rebound strategy. Downsizing a business, particularly laying off employees who have been with the company many years, is painful to everyone. Downsizing means management has, to some extent, thrown in the towel and given up on finding alternatives for maintaining the size of the business and growing. But isn't this exactly one of the core functions of top management—to know how to move the business forward into the future?

Red Ink and Cash Flow

Since we're discussing business decline, this is the appropriate place to bring up an unpleasant subject. What happens to cash flow when the bottom line of the income statement is in red ink? What happens to cash flow from operating activities when there is no profit, but a *loss* for the year? Of course a loss means that expenses were more than sales revenue for the year. As we have examined in this and previous chapters, actual cash inflow during the year from sales revenue is different from the amount of sales revenue. And actual cash outflow during the year for expenses is different from the total amount of expenses.

In most cases, a large loss for the year is due to huge write-downs of assets (or by recording a large liability for future cost obligations). For example, a large part or perhaps even all of the balance in a company's goodwill asset account is written down because the asset suffered what is called *impairment*. This means that management has come to the conclusion that the asset has a smaller future value to the business, or perhaps no value at all. The asset write-down does not involve a cash outlay. So, cash flow from operating activities is not hurt by such an asset write-down. An asset write-down is much like recording depreciation expense, except that the write-down is a one-time charge-off.

Suppose, however, that the bottom-line loss for the year does not involve any asset write-downs (or any liability write-ups). In other words, only regular recurring expenses are deducted from sales revenue, and the total of these normal expenses is more than the total sales revenue for the year. In this situation cash flow from operating activities could be negative. In brief, it's quite possible that total cash outlays for expenses would be more than total cash inflow from sales revneue.

The business in this situation is using up its available cash. The rate at which the business is using up its cash is called the *burn rate*. The burn rate is used to estimate how long the business can live without a major cash infusion. Start-up business ventures typically experience negative operating cash flow during their first few years. Often their burn rate is too high and they don't make it.

16

FOOTNOTES—THE FINE PRINT IN FINANCIAL REPORTS

Financial Statements—Brief Review

The guts of an annual financial report are the three primary financial statements explained in previous chapters. To review briefly:

1. ***Income Statement:*** This is the summary of a company's sales revenue and expenses for the year (the profit-making activities of the business) and, of course, it reports the company's final profit or *net income* for the year. A publicly owned business corporation must report *earnings per share* in its income statement. A nonpublic company doesn't have to report earnings per share, but it is useful information to its shareholders.

2. ***Balance Sheet:*** Also called the statement of financial condition, this is a summary of the company's assets, liabilities, and owners' equity at the close of business on the last day of the income statement period. To understand a balance sheet you need to understand the differences between the basic types of assets used by a business (inventory versus property, plant, and equipment, for instance), and the difference between operating liabilities (mainly accounts payable and accrued expenses) versus debt on which the business pays interest. Also, you should know the difference between the two different sources of owners' equity—capital invested by the owners in the business versus profit earned but not distributed to owners, which is called *retained earnings*.

3. ***Statement of Cash Flows:*** Profit generates cash flow, but the amount of cash flow from profit during the year generally is not equal to net income for the year. This third financial statement starts with a section summarizing cash flow from profit for the year, which is an extremely important number. The statement also reports other sources of cash for the year and what the company did with its available cash during the year. The cash flow statement exposes the financial strategy of the business.

In short, the three financial statements revolve around the three financial imperatives of every business—to make profit, to remain in healthy financial condition, and to make good use of cash flow. The three financial statements usually fit on three pages of an annual financial report, one statement on each page.

Although generally accepted accounting principles (GAAP) do not strictly require it, most businesses—large and small—present two-year or three-year *comparative* financial statements. This permits easy comparison of the year just ended with last year and the year before that. The federal agency that regulates financial reporting by public corporations, the Securities and Exchange Commission, requires comparative financial statements. More than 10,000 public companies are audited by the largest four certified public accountant (CPA) firms (called the Big Four, which used to be the Big Eight not too many years ago before mergers and the demise of Arthur Andersen). Chapter 17 explains audits.

Why Footnotes?

A typical annual report contains more than the basic three financial statements. This chapter focuses on one additional piece of information in annual financial reports—footnotes to financial statements. Footnotes provide the so-called fine print. Without footnotes financial statements would be incomplete, and possibly misleading. Footnotes are an essential supplement to financial statements.

Top-level managers should never forget that they are responsible for the company's financial statements *and* the accompanying footnotes. The footnotes are an integral, inseparable part of the financial statements. In fact, financial statements state this fact on the bottom of each page, usually worded as follows:

> The accompanying footnotes to the financial statements are an integral part of these statements.

The auditor's report (see the next chapter) covers footnotes as well as the financial statements. In short, footnotes are necessary for *adequate disclosure* in financial reports. The overarching concept of financial reporting is adequate disclosure, so that all those who have a legitimate interest in the financial affairs of the business are provided the relevant information they need to make informed decisions and to protect their interests in the business.

Not only should a financial report provide adequate disclosure, but the information should be presented in an understandable manner and every effort should be made to use language and visual layouts and exhibits that are clear and reasonably easy to follow. In other words, financial reports should be transparent. The lack of *transparency* in financial reports has come in for much criticism-especially regarding footnotes that are so dense and obtuse that even a lawyer would have trouble reading them.

Two Types of Footnotes

Footnotes are of two kinds. First, the main accounting methods used by the business are identified and briefly explained. For instance, the particular accounting method used to determine the company's cost of goods sold expense and its ending inventory cost is identified (Chapter 20 explains these methods).

For many expenses and even for sales revenue most businesses can choose between two or three generally accepted accounting methods. The company's selections of accounting methods have to be made clear in footnotes. A footnote is needed for each significant accounting choice by the business. Footnotes assume some familiarity with accounting terminology, as you can see in the footnote from Caterpillar's financial statements quoted here.

A footnote from a recent annual report of Caterpillar Inc. regarding its inventory accounting method reads as follows (from page A-8 of Caterpillar's electronic filing of its 2002 10-K form with the Securities and Exchange Commission):

> Inventories are stated at the lower of cost or market. Cost is principally determined using the last-in, first-out (LIFO) method. The value of inventories on the LIFO basis represented about 80% of total inventories at December 31, 2002, 2001, and 2000.
>
> If the FIFO (first-in, first-out) method had been in use, inventories would have been $1,977, $1,923, and $2,065 higher than reported at December 31, 2002, 2001 and 2000, respectively.

[*Note:* Dollar amounts are reported in millions in Caterpillar's annual report.]

This footnote reveals that Caterpillar's inventories in its balance sheets at these year-ends would have been about $2 billion higher if the company had selected an alternative accounting method. And its cost of goods sold expense for each year would have been different (but "only" by a few million dollars).

Companies disclose their choice of depreciation and amortization methods in footnotes. (Chapter 21 discusses different depreciation methods). For example, Caterpillar's footnote reads:

> Depreciation of plant and equipment is computed principally using accelerated methods. Amortization of purchased intangibles is computed using the straight-line method, generally over a period of 15 years or less. Accumulated amortization was $47, $32, and $21 at December 31, 2002, 2001, and 2000, respectively.

[*Note:* Dollar amounts are reported in millions in Caterpillar's annual report.]

Other common footnotes explain the *consolidation* of the company's financial statements. Many large businesses consist of a family of corporations under the control of one parent company. The financial statements of each corporation are grouped together in one integrated set of financial statements. Intercorporate dealings are eliminated as if there were only one entity. Affiliated companies in which the business has made investments are not consolidated if the company does not have a controlling interest in the other business.

The second type of footnotes provide additional disclosure that cannot be placed in the main body of the financial statements. For example, the maturity dates, interest rates, collateral, or other security provisions, and many other details of the long-term debt of a business are presented in footnotes. Annual rentals required under long-term operating leases are given. Details regarding stock options and employee stock ownership plans are spelled out, and the potential dilution effects on earnings per share are illustrated in footnotes. Major lawsuits and other legal actions against the company are discussed in footnotes.

Details about the company's employees' retirement and pension plans are also disclosed in footnotes. Obligations of the business to pay for postretirement health and medical costs of retired employees are presented in footnotes. The list of possible footnotes is a long one. In preparing its annual report, a business needs to go down a long checklist of items that may have to be disclosed, and then write the footnotes. This is no easy task. The business has to explain in a relatively short space what can be rather complex.

Management Discretion in Writing Footnotes

Managers have to rely on the experts—the chief financial officer of the organization, legal counsel, and the outside CPA auditor—to go through the checklist of footnotes that may be required. Once every required footnote has been identified, key decisions still have to be made regarding each footnote. Managers have much discretion or flexibility regarding just how candid to be and how much detail to reveal in each footnote.

Clearly managers should not give away the farm—they should not divulge information that would damage a competitive advantage the business enjoys. Managers don't have to help their competitors. The idea is to help the company's debtholders and stockholders—to report to them information they're entitled to.

But, just how much information do the debtholders and stockholders need or are they legally entitled to? This is a very difficult question to answer in straightforward and clear-cut terms. Beyond certain basic facts, exactly what should be put in a footnote for "fair" disclosure is not always clear and definite.

Too little disclosure, such as withholding information about a major lawsuit against the business, would be misleading and the top executives of the business would be liable for this lack of disclosure. Beyond the "legal minimum," which should be insisted on by the company's CPA auditors, footnote disclosure rules and guidelines are vague and murky. Managers have rather broad freedom of choice regarding how frank to be and how to express what they put in footnotes.

Opaque Footnotes: A Serious Problem

One point that I must call to your attention concerns the readability of footnotes in general. As an author I may be overly sensitive to this, but I think not. Many investors and securities analysts complain about the dense fog in footnotes. Footnote writing can be so obtuse that you have to suspect that the writing is deliberately obscure. The rules require footnotes, but the rules do not demand that the footnotes be clear and concise so that an average financial report reader can understand them.

Frequently the sentence structure of footnotes seems intentionally legalistic and awkward. Technical terminology abounds in footnotes. Poor writing seems more prevalent in footnotes on sensitive matters, such as lawsuits or ventures that the business abandoned with heavy losses. A lack of candor is obvious in many footnotes.

Creditors and stockholders cannot expect managers to expose all the dirty linen of the business in footnotes, or to confess all their bad decisions. But, better clarity and more frankness certainly would help and would not damage the business.

Some companies go to great efforts to be frank and clear, and even entertaining in their footnotes and other disclosures in their annual financial reports. A model for companies to emulate, in my opinion, are the annual financial reports of Berkshire Hathaway. The chief executive officer and principal stockholder of the company, Warren Buffett, takes pride in his financial reports, as well he should. The reports are delightful to read and are very informative.

True, stockholders can ask top managers and the board of directors questions at the annual meetings of the business. However, managers can be just as evasive in their answers as in their footnotes.

In short, creditors and investors frequently are stymied by poorly written footnotes. You really have only one option, and that's to plow through the underbrush of troublesome footnotes, more than once if necessary. Usually you can tell if particular footnotes are important enough to deserve this extra effort.

17

CPAs, AUDITS, AND AUDIT FAILURES

Why Audits?

Suppose you have invested a fair amount of money in a privately owned business. You are not involved in managing the company; you're an absentee owner—a passive investor. Being a stockholder you receive the company's financial reports, of course. You read the financial statements and footnotes to find out how the company is doing, and whether there might be any storm clouds on the horizon.

Let me ask you a question here: How do you know whether the company's financial statements provide adequate disclosure and whether the business uses approved accounting methods to measure its profit? Do you just presume this? Are you sure you can trust the company's financial reports?

Or, suppose you are a bank loan officer. A business includes its latest financial statements in the loan application package. Does the business use proper accounting methods to prepare its financial statements? Have, perhaps, the financial statements been tweaked for purposes of securing the loan, to make them look better than they really are? It's not unheard-of, you know.

Or, suppose you're a mutual fund investment manager in charge of a large portfolio of stocks traded on the New York Stock Exchange and Nasdaq. Market values of stock shares depend on the net income and earnings per share amounts reported by companies in their financial reports. How do you know that their profit numbers are reliable?

Financial statements can have errors or be misleading for two basic reasons:

1. *Honest mistakes* happen because a company's accounting system is inadequate and fails to detect and correct errors, or because the company's accountants simply do not have adequate understanding of current accounting and financial reporting requirements and standards.

2. *Deliberate dishonesty* happens when employees or top-level managers intentionally distort the company's profit performance and financial statements, or withhold vital information that should be disclosed in the financial report. This is called *financial reporting fraud* or *accounting fraud*.

Erroneous accounting and accounting fraud are ever-present dangers in financial statements. One way to protect against these potentially serious problems is to *audit* the accounting system and records of a business to ascertain whether the company's financial statements are free of errors and adhere to generally accepted accounting principles (GAAP). An audit provides assurance that the company's financial report is reliable and follows the rules. Audits of financial reports are done by independent certified public accountants, a profession we turn to next.

Certified Public Accountants

A person needs to do three things to become a certified public accountant (CPA). He or she must earn a college degree with a fairly heavy major (emphasis) in accounting courses. The American Institute of Certified Public Accountants has strongly encouraged all states to enact laws requiring five years of education. Most but not all states have passed such laws. However, some states—notably California at the time of this writing—have not enacted such laws.

Second, a person must pass the national CPA exam, which is a rigorous two-day exam testing knowledge in accounting, income tax, auditing, and business law. Third, a person must satisfy the experience requirement of the state in which he or she lives. State laws and regulations differ regarding the time and nature of public accounting experience that a person must have; one year is the general minimum.

After the three requirements are completed—education, exam, and experience—the person receives a license by his or her state of residence to practice as a CPA. No one else may hold himself or herself out to the public as a CPA. Most states (perhaps all, but I haven't checked this out) require 30 or 40 hours of continuing education a year to renew a person's CPA license. Every state has a Board of Accountancy that has the duty to regulate the practice of public accounting and the power to revoke or suspend the licenses of individuals who violate the laws, regulations, and ethics governing CPAs.

CPAs do more than just audit financial reports. They offer an ever-widening range of services to the public—income tax compliance and planning, and consulting in areas such as personal financial planning, business valuation, computer systems and information technology, production control and efficiency, and many other fields of specialization. Indeed, nonaudit services used to be a major revenue source of large CPA firms.

The CPA license is widely recognized and respected as a professional credential. The professional status of CPAs rests on their expertise and experience, and their independence from any one client. The word "certified" in their title refers to their expertise and experience. The term "public" refers to their independence. For doing audits of financial statements the independence of CPAs is absolutely essential. To be independent a CPA must be in public practice and not be an employee of any organization (other than the CPA firm itself, of course).

Public accounting experience is a good stepping-stone to other career opportunities. Many persons start in public accounting and end up as the controller (chief accountant), financial vice president, or chief financial officer (CFO) of an organization; some even become presidents and chief executive officers (CEOs) of business organizations. Some CPAs go into politics (a few have become state governors). Persons who have left public accounting are still referred to as CPAs even though they are not in public practice any longer. This is like a person with an M.D. degree who leaves the practice of medicine but is still called "doctor."

Are Audits Required, or Just a Good Idea?

Corporations whose debt and stock securities are traded publicly are required by federal securities law to have their annual financial reports audited by an independent CPA firm. At the time of this writing the four large international CPA firms audit more than 10,000 companies in the United States. Beyond these large public companies, relatively few businesses are *legally* required to have their financial statements audited by independent CPAs.

It has been estimated that there are more than 8.5 million business corporations, partnerships, and limited liability companies, as well as several million sole proprietorships (one-owner business ventures). Not very many of these business entities are required to have audits. Nevertheless, a business may decide to have its financial reports audited even though federal or state securities laws do not apply.

I served on the board of directors (and was a stockholder) of a privately owned bank, and we had CPA audits every year. Lawyers should be consulted regarding state corporation and securities laws; an audit may be required in certain situations. A business may sign a contract or agree informally to have its annual financial reports audited as a condition of borrowing money or when issuing capital stock to new investors in the business.

As just mentioned, large public corporations have no choice; they are legally required, to have audits of their annual financial reports by independent CPA firms. But, if not required, should a business hire a CPA firm to audit its annual financial report?

What's the payoff? Basically, an audit adds credibility to the financial report of a business. Audited financial reports have a higher credibility index than unaudited statements.

Audits by CPAs provide insurance against misleading financial statements. Auditors are expert accounting system detectives, and they thoroughly understand accounting principles and financial reporting standards. Being independent of a business, the CPA auditor will not tolerate fraud in the financial report. But, see the later section in this chapter "Accounting Fraud and Audits" (page 119).

Audits don't come cheap. CPAs are professionals who command high fees. A business cannot ask for a "once-over lightly" audit at a cut rate. An audit is an audit. CPAs are bound by generally accepted auditing standards (GAAS)—the authoritative guidelines in doing audits. There is no such thing as a "bargain basement" audit, or a quick-and-dirty audit that only skims over a company's accounting records. Violations of GAAS can result in lawsuits against the CPA and may damage the CPA's professional reputation.

An audit takes a lot of time because the CPA has to examine a great deal of evidence and make many tests of the accounting records of the business before the CPA is able to express an opinion on the company's financial statements. This time requirement causes the relatively high cost of an audit. A business manager, assuming an audit is not legally required, has to ask whether the gain in credibility is worth the cost of an audit.

A bank may insist on audits as a condition of making loans to a business. The outside (nonmanagement) stockholders of a business may insist on annual audits to protect their investments in the business. In these situations the audit fee is a cost of using outside capital. In many situations, however, outside investors and creditors do not insist on audits. Even so, a business may choose to have an audit as a checkup on its accounting system. A business may decide it needs to have a security check—an independent examination focusing on whether the business is vulnerable to fraud and embezzlement schemes.

There is always a chance of embezzlement and fraud by employees or managers who take advantage of their positions—for example, accepting kickbacks or other under-the-table payments from customers and vendors. Employee theft and dishonesty are, unfortunately, rather prevalent. A financial report audit *may* uncover theft and fraud. However, the detection of fraud is *not* the main purpose for auditing financial reports, even though many people are under the false impression that this is the primary purpose of an audit. It is not.

CPA auditors are required to plan their audit procedures to search for possible fraud and to identify weak internal controls that would allow fraud to go undetected. This is a side benefit of audits; but the main purpose of an audit is to express an opinion on the fairness of financial statements (including footnotes), and whether the financial statements adhere to generally accepted accounting principles.

Fraud would undermine the integrity of the financial statements, of course, so the CPA auditor has to be on the lookout for fraud of all types (as well as for accounting errors). But the CPA says nothing at all about fraud in the audit report. There is no statement such as "we looked for fraud but didn't find any." What the CPA auditor does say is discussed next.

Audit Reports: Clean and Not So Clean Opinions

First of all, let's be clear on one point. I'm talking about *audits of financial reports by CPAs*. There are many other types of audits, such as an audit of your income tax return by the Internal Revenue Service (IRS), audits of federally supported programs by the General Accounting Office, audits within an organization by its own internal auditors, and so on. The following discussion concerns audits by CPAs of financial reports prepared by a business that are released to the outside world—primarily to its owners and others who have a legitimate right to receive a copy of its financial report.

Financial report readers are not too concerned about how an audit is done, nor should they be. The bottom line to them is the opinion of the CPA auditor. They should read the opinion carefully, although there is evidence that most don't or at best just give it a quick glance. Evidently, many financial report users simply assume that having the financial report audited is, by itself, an adequate safeguard. They may assume that the CPA would not be associated with any financial report that is incorrect or misleading.

Many financial report readers seem to assume that if the CPA firm gives an opinion and thereby is associated with a financial report, then the financial statements and footnotes must be okay and are not seriously wrong in any respect. Doesn't the CPA's opinion constitute a stamp of approval? No, not necessarily!

The CPA profession over the years has gone to great lengths to differentiate audit opinions. You've heard the old saying: "If you've seen one, you've seen them all." This is not true about audit opinions. You must read the auditor's report to find out which type of opinion the auditor is giving on the financial statements.

The best audit opinion is called an *unqualified* opinion, or more popularly a "clean" opinion. Exhibit 17.1 on page 115 presents a typical audit report, in this instance for the Microsoft Corporation. Its auditor is Deloitte & Touche, one of the Big Four CPA firms. The first three paragraphs constitute the standard language of a clean, or *unqualified* audit report. In this particular situation the auditor adds a fourth paragraph, to call attention to the adoption of new accounting methods by the company during the periods covered by the audits. This fourth paragraph does not compromise or diminish the auditor's clean opinion on the company's financial statements.

Basically, this opinion states that the CPA has no material disagreements with the financial report. In other words, the CPA attests that the financial statements have been prepared according to generally accepted accounting principles (GAAP) and that the footnotes plus other information in the financial report provide adequate disclosure. (These standards still leave management a wide range of choices, which the next chapter explores.)

In a clean opinion the CPA auditor says, in effect, "I don't disagree with the financial report." The actual wording is: "In our opinion, . . . [the] financial statements present fairly, in all material respects, the financial position of Microsoft Corporation. . . ." The CPA might have prepared the financial statements differently and might have written the footnotes

EXHIBIT 17.1—AUDITOR'S STANDARD OPINION ON FINANCIAL STATEMENTS

INDEPENDENT AUDITOR'S REPORT

To the Board of Directors and Stockholders of Microsoft Corporation:

We have audited the accompanying consolidated balance sheet of Microsoft Corporation and subsidiaries (the Company) as of June 30, 2001 and 2002, and the related consolidated statements of income, cash flows, and stockholders' equity for each of the three years in the period ended June 30, 2002. These financial statements are the responsibility of the Company's management. Our responsibility is to express an opinion on these financial statements based on our audits.

We conducted our audits in accordance with auditing standards generally accepted in the United States of America. These standards required that we plan and perform the audit to obtain reasonable assurance about whether the financial statements are free of material misstatement. An audit includes examining, on a test basis, evidence supporting the amounts and disclosures in the financial statements. An audit also includes assessing the accounting principles used and significant estimates made by management, as well as evaluating the overall financial statement presentation. We believe that our audits provide a reasonable basis for our opinion.

In our opinion, such consolidated financial statements present fairly, in all material respects, the financial position of Microsoft Corporation and subsidiaries as of June 30, 2001 and 2002, and the results of their operations and their cash flows for each of the three years in the period ended June 30, 2002 in conformity with accounting principles generally accepted in the United States of America.

As mentioned in Note 2 to the financial statements the Company adopted Statement of Financial Accounting Standards No. 133, *Accounting for Derivative Instruments and Hedging Activities*, effective July 1, 2000, and Statement of Financial Accounting Standards No. 142, *Goodwill and Other Intangible Assets*, effective July 1, 2001.

/Signed/ DELOITTE & TOUCHE LLP
Deloitte & Touche LLP
Seattle, Washington
July 18, 2002

differently. In fact, the CPA might prefer that different accounting methods had been used. All the CPA states in a clean opinion is that the accounting and disclosure presented in the financial report are acceptable.

The wording of the first three paragraphs of the clean (unqualified) audit report shown in Exhibit 17.1 on page 115 has been the standard wording for many years. It was adopted for several reasons, one of which was to emphasize that the company's management has the primary responsibility for preparing the financial report. This point is mentioned in the first paragraph.

Also, the accounting profession thought that it should be made clear that an audit provides reasonable but not absolute assurance that "the financial statements are free of material misstatement." And it was thought that users of financial reports should be told briefly what an audit involves (the second paragraph in Exhibit 17.1).

The standard version of the CPA auditor's report runs more than 200 words of fairly technical jargon, and demands a lot from the reader, in my opinion. Frankly, the changes over the years in the language of auditor reports were motivated primarily by the surge in lawsuits against auditors. As discussed more fully later in the chapter, some audits failed to catch fraudulent financial statements; the CPA firms gave clean opinions on financial statements that later were discovered to be seriously misleading because of management fraud, or were based on accounting methods that in hindsight proved to be indefensible.

The rash of audit failures during recent years has received extensive headline-level coverage in the media, which makes it difficult to step back from all the hullabaloo to keep a balanced perspective on things. A later section in the chapter ("Accounting Fraud and Audits," on page 119) takes a closer look at audit failures. The overall rate of audit failures, although very difficult to determine with any precise objectivity, appears to be quite low.

You could count up perhaps 100 major accounting fraud cases over the past decade. This number of audit failures should be compared against more than 10,000 publicly owned businesses that issued audited financial reports over the decade. Therefore, relatively few publicly owned businesses engaged in accounting fraud over this time period. The large majority of businesses are honest in their financial reporting, or at least they have no reason to misstate their financial statements.

The cost of making all audits fail-safe would be prohibitive. In the grand scheme of things a few audit failures are tolerated in order to keep the overall cost of audits within reason. In moments of deep cynicism it has occurred to me that perhaps the real reason for audits is to provide creditors and investors someone to sue when they suffer losses and there is evidence that the company's financial reports were deficient or misleading.

When a business has to go back after the fact and restate its financial statements, or when because of misleading financial reporting the company ends up with serious legal problems, stock investors and creditors usually lose money. So, they look around for someone to sue to recover some of their losses. CPA firms that have deep pockets are a convenient target. Because of this the public accounting profession decided to adopt more defensive language in their audit reports, to better cover their backsides when they are sued. I believe that the auditing profession, notwithstanding its legal problems, has lost sight of the users of financial reports.

The vast majority of financial report users, in my opinion, simply want to know whether the CPA has any objection to the financial statements and footnotes prepared by management. They don't care that much about the specific wording used in the CPA auditor's report. They want to know one thing: Does the

CPA auditor give his or her blessing to management's financial report? If not, they want the CPA auditor to make clear his or her objections to the financial report.

Financial report users should look at the CPA auditor's report to see first, whether the auditor gives a clean opinion, and second, whether the auditor provides any additional information. Often the standard, three-paragraph audit report is expanded in the following situations:

- The CPA auditor wants to emphasize one or more points, such as related-party transactions reported in the financial statements, significant events during the year, unusual uncertainties facing the business, or other matters.

- The company has changed its accounting methods between the most recent year and previous years, which causes inconsistencies with the originally issued financial reports of the business.

- There is substantial doubt about the entity's ability to continue as a going concern, because of financial difficulties in meeting the due dates for payment of its liabilities, or because of other large liabilities it may not be able to pay.

Creditors and investors should be informed in these situations, so the audit profession has decided that these matters should be mentioned explicitly in the auditor's report. Such additional information in the audit report does not constitute a qualification on the company's financial report; it just provides more information.

In contrast, the CPA auditor may have to take exception to an accounting method used by the company, or the lack of disclosure for some item that the CPA thinks is necessary for adequate disclosure. In this situation the CPA renders a *qualified* opinion

that includes the key words "except for" in the opinion paragraph. The grounds for the qualification (what the auditor takes exception to) are explained in the auditor's report. To give a qualified opinion the CPA auditor must be satisfied that taken as a whole the financial report of the company is not misleading. Nevertheless, the CPA disagrees with one or more items in the financial report, especially if the company has departed from generally accepted accounting principles.

The Securities and Exchange Commission (SEC) generally will not accept qualified audit opinions, because the company could change its accounting or disclosure to avoid the auditor's qualified opinion. On the other hand, a qualified opinion may be due to a limitation on the scope of the CPA's examination; the CPA was not able to gather evidence for one or more accounts in the financial statements, and therefore has to qualify or restrict his or her opinion with regard to the items not examined. This sort of qualified opinion may be accepted by the SEC as the best the CPA auditor could do in the circumstances.

How serious a matter is a qualified opinion? Basically, a qualified opinion has a "fly in the ointment" effect. The auditor points out a flaw in the company's financial report, but not a fatal flaw. A qualified audit opinion is a yellow flag, but not a red flag.

One thing to remember: The CPA auditor must be of the opinion that the overall fairness of the financial report is satisfactory, even though there are one or more deviations from established accounting and disclosure standards. If the auditor is of the opinion that the deviations are so serious as to make the financial statements misleading, then the CPA must issue an *adverse* opinion. You hardly ever see an adverse opinion. No business wants to put out misleading financial statements and have the CPA auditor say so for everyone to see!

The CPA auditor may have to *disclaim* an opinion due to limitations on the scope of the audit or due to very unusual uncertainties facing the business. In some situations a CPA may have very serious disagreements with the client that cannot be resolved to the auditor's satisfaction. The CPA may withdraw from the engagement (i.e., walk off the audit). This is not very common, but it happens every now and then. In these situations the CPA has to notify top management, the board of directors of the company, and its audit committee members and make clear the nature of the disagreements and why the CPA is withdrawing from the audit.

The CPA does not act as a whistle-blower beyond the inner confines of the company. For public companies, the CPA has to inform the SEC that the firm has withdrawn from the audit engagement and whether there were any unresolved disagreements between the CPA and the company.

Accounting Fraud and Audits

To jack up market prices so they could make millions of dollars off their stock options, the management of many businesses allegedly resorted to *cooking the books*. The more correct term for this is *accounting fraud*. The word *fraud* means deception and deceit, which is doubly bad if done by a person in a position of trust and authority. Over the past few years an incredible number of management accounting fraud cases have been splashed across the media—WorldCom, Enron, Tyco, Ahold, Xerox, Rite Aid, Global Crossing, HealthSouth, Waste Management, Adelphia Communications, and many more, I'm sad to say. The financial statements of all these companies were audited.

The market prices of these corporations' stock shares plunged and their shareholders suffered huge losses. Unfortunately, many employees of these companies had the bulk of their retirement savings invested in their companies' stock shares. Many of these businesses went into bankruptcy. I was astonished at the large number of accounting frauds. We've had accounting frauds over the years—in the 1930s and a rash in the 1960s. Then the frauds were like a few blemishes on your face; in the past few years they have been like a bad case of acne.

The auditors of the companies that allegedly cooked their books were the Big Five CPA firms, presumably the best auditors in the world. One firm—Arthur Andersen—was convicted of obstruction of justice for destroying evidence in the Enron case. Almost overnight Andersen ceased to audit publicly owned companies; thousands of its professional staff had to find jobs with other CPA firms or change their careers. The remaining Big Four CPA firms face lawsuits and regulatory sanctions for failing to discover the alleged financial reporting fraud by their audit clients.

Like most persons, I'm outraged by the unbridled greed and gaping lack of rectitude of top-level managers who allegedly orchestrated these accounting fraud schemes. Those who cooked their books should stew in their own juices. Whether any of them will serve jail time is doubtful. The first survival rule of a thief is to not get caught. Indeed, some white-collar crooks got away with their scams for many years while accumulating their illegitimate fortunes.

Cooking the books means making false accounting entries or deliberately not making accounting entries that should be recorded. The purpose is to show profit (bottom-line net income) when in fact the business actually has a loss or has actually earned far less profit than recorded in the books based on the bogus accounting entries. The basic ways of cooking the books are: Sales revenue is recorded for "sales" that haven't been made. Costs that have been paid for expenses are recorded as asset increases instead of as expenses. Liabilities for expenses are not recorded. Asset write-downs that should be recorded as losses are not recorded. There are countless variations on these basic themes for cooking the books.

Keep in mind: Most businesses massage or manipulate their accounting numbers to some extent. A business can select conservative accounting methods that dampen down its profit numbers, or conversely it can adopt aggressive accounting methods that accelerate the recording of profit. But most businesses stay within the boundaries of generally accepted accounting principles. Their accounting methods are aboveboard even though they may be on the edge of accounting rules. Cooking the books, in contrast, crosses the line and is illegitimate. Businesses that cook their books are accounting outlaws.

Quite clearly, CPA auditors do not always discover accounting fraud that is going on right under their noses. Most of the accounting frauds over the past few years were exposed because a key employee blew the whistle, or because the fraud scheme collapsed of its own weight or came apart at the seams. Evidently the auditors were as surprised as anyone. To my knowledge, no one believes that the auditor was in conspiracy with management in any of the recent accounting fraud scandals.

Rather, the prevailing question is: Shouldn't the auditors have discovered these massive accounting frauds? After all, auditors are hired to be financial report detectives; they should carry out their job with professional skepticism and take a hard look at the company's accounting system and methods. They should act like junkyard watchdogs on behalf of the shareholders. Nevertheless, the auditors failed to discover many accounting scams over the past few years.

The Big Four CPA firms protest that they really aren't responsible for detecting high-level management fraud—unless they happen to come across evidence of the fraud through their customary audit procedures. They complain that they are victims of an *expectations gap*; financial report users expect too much from an audit regarding management fraud. If their argument is valid, then I would counterargue that the opinion paragraph in the audit report should begin: "In our opinion, assuming there is no accounting fraud that we haven't discovered, the financial statements present fairly . . ." The audit report includes no such language, of course.

The surge in the number and the large scale of accounting frauds caused Congress to hold hearings and take action. The Sarbanes-Oxley Act of 2002 was signed into law by President George W. Bush. Many radical reforms were instituted by this piece of legislation. The centerpiece of the law was the creation of a new board under the auspices of the Securities and Exchange Commission, called the Public Company Accounting Oversight Board (PCAOB). This new board has very broad powers over accounting and auditors. Many new responsibilities were imposed on corporate management and corporate audit committees. CPA auditors will have to live with many new regulations and with prohibitions on consulting and other services they can offer to their audit clients.

The PCAOB clamped down on consulting and certain other services that CPA firms had in the past provided to their audit clients. The purpose is to avoid a conflict of interest that may exist when a CPA firm sells advice to a client that the firm also audits. When the CPA firm wears both an audit hat and a consulting hat the firm may go easy on the business as its auditor in order to protect its highly profitable consulting fees. Public companies will have to use a different CPA firm than its auditor for consulting and most nonaudit services.

The many accounting fraud scandals over recent years have made one thing very clear: Conventional audit procedures are not enough to ferret out well-conceived, sophisticated accounting fraud perpetrated by high-level managers. The audit team might come across something that arouses their suspicion during the course of a audit—but there's a good chance they won't. The public accounting profession, in my view, hasn't done enough to be clear on this point. Perhaps I'm too harsh. But I think that the fraud detection limits of audits—although discussed in the technical language of official auditing pronouncements—have not been made clear to the general audience of investors and investment professionals.

The official auditing pronouncements stress the need for a business to establish an effective system of internal controls to prevent accounting fraud. But top-level managers can override and circumvent internal controls to carry out their accounting fraud schemes. In short, management is very good at concealing accounting fraud, and auditors are very bad at finding accounting fraud hidden by management.

Management is good at creating disinformation to mislead auditors. When deceived by management, auditors have blinders on and do not know everything they should. In these situations the audit is incomplete, which is comparable to having a physical exam that doesn't include blood tests.

To improve their chances of discovering management accounting fraud, CPAs need to start using new audit procedures that would not be as "client friendly" as present audit procedures. In my view you have to fight fire with fire. Conventional audit procedures fall short of the mark for flushing out accounting fraud perpetrated by high-level managers. However, auditors probably would view these methods as being outside the range of legal and permissible audit procedures.

For example, auditors could contact former employees of the business and ask them whether they have any qualms about the company's accounting methods. Auditors could provide a means for employees of the business who have knowledge about fraud to communicate anonymously and safely with them. Auditors could employ certain espionage and surveillance procedures to search for possible accounting fraud, such as planting an under-cover mole in the business to act as an agent in place who reports to the auditor.

Also, it doesn't help that audits are done under relatively tight cost and time constraints and that a large part of the audit team consists of relatively inexperienced young persons who are not as skeptical as they should be. I always told the students in my auditing classes that to catch a crook you have to think like a crook. But if you're not a crook thinking this way is not easy.

There's always a chance that auditors might discover accounting fraud. Generally accepted auditing standards require that auditors identify high-risk areas and apply procedures to search for possible fraud and errors. On the other hand, management knows what procedures its auditors use in looking for fraud. Management knows not to leave behind any telltale evidence that would tip off the auditors.

I've worked on many audits in which management cooperated fully; there was no evidence of financial reporting fraud, and the company's accounting methods were well within the boundaries of generally accepted accounting principles. I've worked on the other kind of audits as well. In one case we were lucky; we found evidence of management fraud through normal audit procedures (which doesn't usually happen, as mentioned earlier). The managers were a bunch of crooks. In this case our firm walked off the audit.

In other cases we failed to discover major accounting errors and management fraud even though we followed generally accepted auditing standards and procedures. The result sometimes was that the company's financial reports were presented with our blessing (clean opinion). In one unusual case I remember the new senior-in-charge on the job decided that first he would make a tour of the business. He wasn't familiar with the layout of the client's plant and warehouses. None of the employees knew that he was the new auditor. During his walk around he saw evidence of major fraud, which was confirmed through detailed analysis. It certainly helps to know specifically where to look for fraud.

The audit of this privately owned company was done primarily for its bank, which had made substantial loans to the company.

Once the fraud was discovered (it had been going on many years), a deal was worked out. The president of the company, the auditor in charge, and the bank's principal executive agreed that no audit opinion would be given on the company's financial report, even though an audit was done. (As an aside, the IRS caught wind of the fraud and pounced on the company and its managers for tax evasion.)

In the grand scheme of things, the possibility of accounting fraud is one of the risks that investors cannot entirely avoid. Of course it's a good idea to establish and enforce a system that minimizes the risk of accounting fraud, but this might come with a fairly high cost. The recent reforms enacted by the Sarbanes-Oxley Act could be the radical surgery needed to prevent accounting fraud in the future. Or the changes might amount to no more than a face-lift that only makes things look better. We shall see.

Accounting and Review Services by CPAs

A small business may not be able to afford an audit. Bankers and other sources of loans to businesses understand this, so they generally do not insist on audits. However, they may want a CPA to at least look over the financial reports of companies they loan money to; or they may make clear to their small-business customers that they would be more comfortable if the businesses used a CPA to advise them on their financial statements.

A CPA can perform certain limited procedures that are called a *review*. A review is far less than a full-scale audit. But a review provides enough evidence about the company's financial statements so that the CPA can go on record that he or she is not aware of any modifications (changes) that are needed to make the financial statements conform with generally accepted accounting principles.

The CPA warns the financial report readers that a review is substantially less than an audit and that, accordingly, no opinion is being expressed on the company's financial statements. Based on a review, the CPA does not give an affirmative opinion but rather a negative assurance ("no modifications are needed . . ."). This negative assurance may be sufficient to satisfy lenders or investors in the business.

Many smaller businesses need the help of a CPA to prepare their financial statements. A CPA comes in and from the company's accounting records (which may need some adjustments) the CPA prepares the company's financial statements. In this situation the CPA is said to *compile* the financial statements. No audit and no review is done. So, the CPA must disclaim any opinion on the financial statements; and, no negative assurance may be given.

Most smaller businesses use CPAs to prepare their income tax returns and to advise them on how to minimize their income taxes. Also, they turn to CPAs for a wide variety of advice—for example, recommendations on accounting software.

18

CHOOSING ACCOUNTING METHODS AND QUALITY OF EARNINGS

GAAP: The Name of the Game

Financial statements are prepared in conformity with standards that have been established over the years called generally accepted accounting principles (GAAP). Rarely, if ever, would you come across financial statements of a business prepared according to accounting methods other than GAAP. The minor business exceptions to this general comment are not worth mentioning. (Financial statements of nonprofit organizations and government entities follow somewhat different accounting principles and practices.)

Audits by independent certified public accountants (CPAs) are precisely for the purpose of making sure that GAAP have been followed in preparing the financial statements (see Chapter 17). In short, anytime you pick up the financial report of a business you are entitled to assume that its financial statements have been prepared according to GAAP.

The fundamental idea is to provide a well-defined set of general accounting methods and practices that all businesses should follow faithfully for measuring their profits and for presenting their financial conditions and cash flows. The twofold purpose is to have all businesses play by the same accounting rules regarding how they keep score financially and to make financial statements of different businesses comparable with one another. You can imagine the confusion if every business were to choose its own unique accounting methods. For instance, one business may use historical cost basis depreciation and another may use current replacement cost basis depreciation.

The six basic steps in the accounting process of a business are:

1. Identify and analyze all transactions and operations of the business during the period, as well as the developments affecting the business that need to be recognized.

2. Determine the correct accounting methods for transactions, operations, and other developments according to GAAP.

3. Record and accumulate the transactions, operations, and other developments during the period, using the correct accounting methods, of course.

4. At the end of the period assemble the accounts for sales revenue, expenses, assets, liabilities, and owners' equity, and make sure their ending balances are up-to-date and accurate.

5. Prepare the financial statements for the period and write the footnotes for the statements according to the prescribed rules of presentation and disclosure. (Include the CPA's report if the statements have been audited.)

6. Distribute the financial report to everyone entitled to receive a copy.

This chapter focuses on step 2—choosing one of the alternative methods allowed under GAAP for the transactions, operations, and other developments affecting the business.

Suppose, purely hypothetically, that a business employs two equally qualified accountants and neither knows of the other's presence. Suppose both accountants keep the books entirely independent of one another. This company would have two sets of books but only one set of transactions, operations, and developments during the year to account for.

Now the critical question: Would both accountants come up with the same net income (profit) number for the year? Would their ending balance sheets be virtually the same? Would their footnotes be the same? You can probably see what's coming here.

The two accountants, in all likelihood, would come up with *different* net incomes for the year. One or more of their expenses would be different, and their sales revenue for the year also might be different. This means that their balance sheets would be different. Sales revenue and expenses cause increases and decreases in assets and liabilities. So, if expenses are different, then assets and liabilities will be different. And if net income for the year is different, then the retained earnings balance in the ending balance sheet will be different.

Does this mean that one of the company's accountants is wrong and has made mistakes in applying generally accepted accounting principles? No, assume not; neither has made a mistake. Then how can the two of them come up with different accounting numbers? The answer is that for many expenses, and even for sales revenue, the GAAP rule book does not prescribe one and only one accounting method, but allows two or three alternative methods to be used.

Financial accounting would seem to be like measuring a person's weight on a scale that gives correct readings, wouldn't it? But, as a matter of fact, financial accounting according to GAAP allows a business to select which kind of scale to use—one that weighs light or one that weighs heavy.

We can think of the GAAP set of rules as an official cookbook for financial accounting that has more than one recipe for many dishes (expenses and sales revenue). For example, cost of goods sold expense and depreciation expense can be accounted for by different but equally accepted methods. Chapter 16 explains that a company's choices of accounting methods for these two key expenses are disclosed in footnotes to the company's financial statements. Chapter 20 explains cost of goods sold expense methods, and Chapter 21 explains depreciation methods.

This chapter discusses the diversity within GAAP that permits more than one accounting method to be used to record the transactions and operations of a business. The activities of the business are the same, but the accounting for them is different depending on which methods are selected. The financial reporting game can be played using different methods of scorekeeping.

Virtually every business has to pick and choose among different accounting methods for several of its expenses and perhaps for recording its sales revenue as well. For most businesses the profit result is the dominate factor in choosing among accounting methods. How will net income be affected by the choice between accounting methods? This is the main question on the minds of most business managers.

Business Managers and GAAP

Many deplore the "looseness" or "elasticity" of accounting methods that are permitted under the umbrella of generally accepted accounting principles (GAAP)—but not business managers by and large. For one thing, business managers know from experience that almost every law, regulation, guideline, benchmark, standard, or rule is subject to more than one interpretation. Business managers, in other words, are accustomed to operating in a fuzzy world of shades of gray; they don't expect to find clear-cut, black-and-white distinctions very often. I would surmise that the reaction of most business managers to the earlier discussion of GAAP's diversity probably is—"So, what else is new?"

Second, business managers probably welcome having a choice of accounting methods. In fact, they might prefer to have even more choices for their accounting methods and disclosures. The evolution of GAAP over the years has been in the direction of narrowing the range of acceptable accounting methods and reporting practices. Accounting methods have been tightened up over the years. Nevertheless, the Financial Accounting Standards Board (FASB) still issues pronouncements that permit more than one accounting method or more than one manner for disclosing certain matters in financial reports.

The chief executive officer (CEO) of the business as well as its other top-level managers should make certain that the company's financial statements are fairly presented, especially that the accounting methods used to measure the company's profit are within the range of choices permitted by GAAP. If its accounting methods are outside these limits, the company could stand accused of issuing false and misleading financial statements. The managers would be liable for damages suffered by the company's creditors and stockholders who relied on its misleading financial statements. If for no other reason than this, managers should pay close attention to the choices of accounting methods used to prepare their companies' financial statements.

The chief executive officer of the business and its other top-level managers should decide which accounting methods and policies are best for the company. They have to decide between *conservative* (cautious) versus *aggressive* (liberal) profit-accounting methods, which means whether to record profit later (conservative) or sooner (aggressive).

The accounting choices have to do with the *timing* for recording sales revenue and expenses. The sooner sales revenue is recorded, the earlier profit is reported; and the later expenses are recorded, the earlier profit is reported. If a business wants to report profit as soon as possible it should instruct its accountants to choose those accounting methods that accelerate sales revenue and delay expenses.

On the other hand, if a business wants to be conservative it should order its accountants to use those accounting methods that delay the recording of sales revenue and accelerate the recording of expenses, so that profit is reported as late as possible. The accounting methods selected for cost of goods sold expense and depreciation expense are two main examples of conservative versus aggressive methods for recording profit. Chapters 20 and 21 discuss the generally accepted accounting methods for these two key expenses.

Business managers may prefer to avoid getting involved in choosing accounting methods. I think this is a mistake. First, as already mentioned, there is the risk that the financial statements may not be prepared completely in accordance with GAAP, especially if the financial statements are not audited by independent CPAs. Second, top-level managers should adopt those accounting methods that best fit the general policies and philosophy of the business. The CEO should decide which "look" of the financial statements is in the best interests of the business.

Somebody has to choose the accounting methods—if not the managers then by default the company's controller. The controller, being the chief accounting officer of the company, should work hand-in-glove with the CEO and the other top-level managers to make sure that the accounting methods being used by the business are not working at cross-purposes with the goals, objectives, strategies, and plans of the organization.

Consistency of Accounting Methods

Once a business chooses which accounting methods to use for recording its sales revenue and expenses, the business sticks with these methods. A company does not flip-flop between accounting methods. The Internal Revenue Service and the Securities and Exchange Commission take a dim view of switching accounting methods one year to the next. Furthermore, CPA auditors have to mention such changes in their audit reports. Changes may be needed in certain circumstances, but the large majority of businesses don't change their accounting methods except on rare occasions.

Consistency of accounting methods from year to year is very important. As mentioned earlier, the difference between accounting methods has to do with *when* sales revenue and expenses are recorded. Year by year, the annual amounts of sales revenue and expenses differ between accounting methods, and thus bottom-line profit will differ. The amounts of these differences can be very pronounced in the early start-up years of a business or during years of rapid expansion or drastic decline. However, for a mature company that is not experiencing rapid growth or steep decline, the end result in terms of annual net income may be minimal—although it's hard to know for sure.

Generally accepted accounting principles do *not* require that a business determine and report how much different its annual net income would have been if the company had used alternative accounting methods instead of the methods it actually used. Conservative accounting methods can have a very pronounced effect on the cost values reported in a company's balance sheet for its inventory and long-term operating assets. If inventory cost is materially less than current cost values, then a business discloses the difference between the balance sheet cost value of its inventory and the estimated current cost of the inventory.

For example, please refer again to Caterpillar's inventory footnote on page 104 in Chapter 16, which reports that this asset's cost in the company's ending balance sheet is about $2 billion lower under the conservative accounting method it uses, compared with what the cost would have been if the company had used an alternative accounting method. This means that over the years the company reported $2 billion less profit before income tax, which is a lot of money, of course.

Keep in mind, however, that this total difference in the company's ending inventory cost value is the cumulative effect over many years. Caterpillar has been using this accounting method since the 1950s, for more than 50 years. The pretax difference on profit can be determined for each year given the information Caterpillar provides in its footnote. For 2002, for instance, Caterpillar's pretax profit would have been $54 million more under the alternative method, which is about 5% of its $1,142 million consolidated profit before taxes for the year.

Massaging the Numbers and Cooking the Books

Beyond choosing between alternative accounting methods, business managers can go two steps further in manipulating recorded profit. The first technique is called *massaging the numbers* or *income smoothing*. Business managers can control the timing of some expenses and sales revenue to some extent and therefore boost or dampen recorded profit for the year. In this way managers "put a thumb on the scale," the scale being net income for the year. When managers cross the line and go too far it's called *cooking the books*. Cooking the books constitutes accounting fraud—see Chapter 17.

The most common way of massaging the numbers involves the discretionary expenses of a business. Consider repair and maintenance expenses, for instance. Until the work is done, no expense is recorded. A manager can simply move back or move up the work orders for these expenditures, and thus either avoid recording some expense in this period or record more expense in the period. In this way the manager controls the timing of these expenses. There are other discretionary expenses of a business. Two come quickly to mind—employee training and development costs and advertising expenditures.

Managers control the timing of discretionary expenses, it is thought, to smooth profit from period to period. Instead of permitting the profit numbers to pop out of the process of the accounting system and letting the chips fall where they may, a manager may ask the company's controller to let him or her know in advance how profit for the period is shaping up, to get a preview of the final profit number for the year.

The profit lookout for the year may be below or above expectations. The look ahead at profit may indicate an unacceptable swing from last year. In these situations the manager may decide to nudge the profit number up or down, and the best way of doing this is to manipulate discretionary expenses. Or, the manager can control the timing for recording revenues. Sales can be accelerated, for example, by shipping more products to the company's captive dealers even though they didn't order the products. The business is taking away sales from next year to put the sales on the books this year.

Cooking the books is very serious stuff and goes beyond massaging the numbers or doing some profit smoothing. It's fundamentally different from taking advantage of discretionary expenses to give profit a boost up or a shove down. Cooking the books is not just "fluffing the pillows" to make profit look a little better or worse for the period. Cooking the books means that sales revenue is recorded when in fact no sales were made, or that actual expenses or losses during the period are not recorded.

Cooking the books requires falsification of the accounting records. To put it as bluntly as I can, cooking the books constitutes *fraud*—the deliberate design of deceptive financial statements. The section "Accounting Fraud and Audits" in Chapter 17 (page 119) discusses cooking the books in more detail.

Quality of Earnings

You often see the phrase *quality of earnings* in the business and financial press. Reported net income is put to a quality test, or a litmus test as it were. This term does not have a precise definition, but clearly most persons who use this term refer to the quality of the accounting methods used by a business to record its profit.

Conservative accounting methods are generally viewed as high-quality, and aggressive accounting methods are viewed with more caution by stock analysts and professional investment managers. They like to see some margin for safety or some cushion for a rainy day in a company's accounting numbers. They know that many estimates and choices have to be made in financial accounting, and they would just as soon a business err on the low side rather than the high side.

Professional investors and investment managers are especially alert for accounting methods that appear to record revenue (or other sources of income) too early, or that fail to record losses or expenses that should be recognized. Even though the financial statements are audited, investment professionals go over them with a fine-tooth comb to get a better feel for how trustworthy are the reported earnings of a business.

They pay a lot of attention to cash flow from profit (operating activities) because this is one number managers cannot manipulate—the business either got the cash flow or it didn't. Accounting methods determine profit, but not cash flow. If reported profit is backed up with steady cash flow, stock analysts rate the quality of earnings very high.

To think that financial reports issued by businesses are pure as driven snow is naive. People are people, after all; we're not all angels. As my father-in-law puts it, "There's a little larceny in everyone's heart." Just because a few cops accept bribes doesn't mean all police are on the take. Clearly the large majority of businesses prepare honest financial statements. But there are some crooks in business, and they are not above preparing false financial statements.

19

MAKING AND CHANGING ACCOUNTING STANDARDS

Why Financial Statements Are So Important

Millions of persons depend on financial statements for vital information about the profit (or loss) performance, financial condition, and cash flows of businesses. This sweeping congregation of financial report users includes bankers deciding whether to make loans to businesses; investors deciding whether to buy, hold, or sell stocks and bonds of public corporations; buyers and sellers of businesses deciding the value of companies; owners of closely held businesses evaluating how their ventures are doing; suppliers deciding whether to sell to businesses on credit; and pension fund managers carrying out their fiduciary responsibility, which requires due diligence in managing other people's money.

For that matter, what about *business managers*? Managers are the first and most immediate users of financial statements. Managers depend on their income statements to know how much profit was made (or how much loss was incurred). Managers also need balance sheet and cash flow information to keep on top of the financial condition of the business, to spot any solvency problems that may be developing, and to plan for the capital requirements of the business.

In short, both insiders and outsiders need dependable financial statements that are designed for and meet the needs and interests of the users of these sources of financial information.

Financial statements are the *primary* and *only direct* source of information for the profit performance of a business, and for its financial condition and cash flow information. Other sources of financial information about a company are *secondary* sources, which pass along information reported in the company's financial statements. Public businesses put out press releases announcing their latest earnings performance but these are preliminary and subject to later confirmation in their financial reports.

It goes without saying that financial statements should be reliable and meet the information demands of users. Financial statement users generally are interested in three main things about a business:

1. Its *profit (or loss) performance*.

2. Its *financial condition* and in particular the *solvency prospects* of the company, which refers to the ability of the business to pay its liabilities on time and to avoid getting into financial trouble.

3. Its *capitalization (ownership) structure*, which refers to the one or more classes of capital stock shares issued by the company, whether any debt of the company can be converted into capital stock, the number of capital stock options given to managers and employees including the terms of the options, and any other direct or indirect claims that participate in the profit of the business.

Investors and other users may seek additional information in the financial statements of a business—such as whether it has enough cash in the bank plus future cash flow to provide for growth. But the three items just listed constitute the hard core of information users look for in financial statements.

This chapter looks at the accounting rules that govern profit measurement and financial statement disclosure. Financial statements are no better than the standards that are used to prepare the statements. As mentioned earlier, these rules are called generally accepted accounting principles (GAAP), and include both accounting methods and disclosure requirements. How good are the rules? Are GAAP changed from time to time?

I think an outside observer surveying the scene would conclude that the financial reporting system works well, and therefore the rules (generally accepted accounting principles) are adequate to the purpose and functions of financial statements. On the other hand, a rumble of criticism persists that has not subsided over the years. Perhaps expectations of financial statement users have risen. Perhaps financial accounting can't keep up with the growing complexity and sophistication of the business and economic environment.

This chapter takes a critical look at GAAP, the governing rules of financial reporting. The following discussion is meant in a friendly sense; the critical remarks that follow assume that the present state of affairs is sound and works reasonably well. However, the present system is not perfect and some improvements could be made.

GAAP and the FASB, SEC, AICPA, IASB and PCAOB

Sorry for all these acronyms. But you see them often in the financial press, especially in articles discussing accounting standards and financial reporting.

The bedrock premise for external financial reporting by a business is that its financial statements and footnotes must be prepared in accordance with generally accepted accounting principles (GAAP). In the United States the dominant authoritative body for GAAP is the Financial Accounting Standards Board (FASB). Its work is supplemented by two key committees of the American Institute of Certified Public Accountants (AICPA), which fill in gaps not dealt with by the FASB.

The Public Company Accounting Oversight Board (PCAOB) was created by the Sarbanes-Oxley Act of 2002, which was passed by Congress in reaction to many audit failures during the past several years. These audits failed to discover enormous accounting frauds. I've already touched on this important piece of federal legislation in Chapter 17—see "Accounting Fraud and Audits" on page 119.

The Sarbanes-Oxley Act deals mainly with improving the quality of audits and the independence of CPA auditors. It might have been better to call the board the "Public Company *Auditing* Oversight Board." The PCAOB was given broad powers and will have the dominant role in regulating the auditing profession. Indeed, the Act can be viewed as the result of the inability of the auditing profession to police itself over the years. Many pious standards were adopted by the auditing profession. The actual practice of some of the Big Five (now the Big Four) CPA firms fell short of these lofty standards. Congress was in no mood to hear any more excuses and promises.

The Sarbanes–Oxley Act also imposes new financial reporting duties on corporate management. The CEO has to certify that his or her company's financial report is presented fairly and is in full compliance with all relevant accounting principles and financial reporting requirements. Also, management is required to state its opinion on the internal controls of the business in the annual financial reports. Furthermore, the Act imposes many new financial disclosure responsibilities on high-level managers.

Members of the PCAOB are appointed by the Securities and Exchange Commission (SEC), after consultation with the chair of the Federal Reserve Board and the Secretary of the Treasury. The SEC retains broad oversight and enforcement authority over the PCAOB and continues to have broad oversight powers over the FASB in its making of authoritative pronouncements on GAAP.

The SEC has the legal basis to take away from the FASB the power to issue authoritative GAAP pronouncements, but it's very unlikely that this will happen. The accounting fraud scandals that led to the Sarbanes-Oxley Act and the creation of the PCAOB had very little to do with the lack of good accounting standards. The accounting standards were in place. The problem was that auditors failed to discover that their clients were violating these standards.

The SEC has in the past overridden and undoubtedly in the future will continue to override the FASB on some matters. Also, the SEC issues many financial reporting requirements that the FASB does not deal with. Nevertheless, the main source of authoritative pronouncements on GAAP for the past generation has been the FASB. The FASB will continue to exercise this role in the foreseeable future.

Many businesses are international in the scope of their operations, as I'm sure you know. Many of these businesses issue financial reports in one or more foreign countries. In times past each country had its own accounting rules—or lack of accounting rules. The International Accounting Standards Board (IASB) was founded in 2001 to establish global accounting principles. Its more specific objective is to establish a comprehensive body of authoritative accounting principles for the European Union (EU). It has issued over 40 pronouncements.

The IASB has been accused of Anglo-American domination and has met with critical reaction to some of its pronouncements. Its overall goal is to bring about the "harmonization" of accounting principles and methods among all economically developed countries. This is a tall order, to say the least.

Changing the Rules

Chapter 18 explains that financial accounting rules are not a straitjacket—GAAP are a little "loose." Generally accepted accounting principles cut managers a fair amount of slack. Managers can select from among alternative profit accounting methods for expenses and sales revenue, and they exercise a fair amount of discretion concerning what is disclosed in their financial reports and how it is written. On the other hand, Chapter 18 also points out that companies have to be consistent and use the same accounting methods year to year.

Are the rules themselves (GAAP) consistent over time? Financial accounting rules remind me of other rules, laws, principles, or standards that have changed over time. Remember when 55 miles per hour was the highway speed limit? I grew up when there was no three-point shot in basketball. Roger Maris and then Mark McGwire, Sammy Sosa, and Barry Bonds broke Babe Ruth's single-season home run record. But their seasons had more games.

Financial accounting rules constantly evolve. Every year the Financial Accounting Standards Board (FASB), the authoritative accounting rule-making body in the United States, introduces new rules; it also amends (or fine-tunes) old rules and issues replacement rules that supersede old rules. It wasn't that long ago, for example, that the cash flow statement was not required and companies did not report it. I was a CPA for 13 years before earnings per share had to be disclosed in financial reports of public corporations.

Financial accounting rules lag instead of lead—rules come out *after* the fact rather than before. First there is a problem; then later a rule is adopted to deal with the problem. A profit accounting problem or a financial reporting disclosure issue develops in actual practice that is not specifically covered in the official rule book of generally accepted accounting principles (GAAP). Criticism continues to mount, but actual accounting and disclosure practices do not respond to the criticism.

Eventually the criticism coalesces into a sufficient consensus of concern that the FASB puts the matter on its agenda. The issue works its way through the due process procedures of the board (which can take a fairly long time). Finally, a pronouncement is issued by the FASB. Often the new rule does not please everyone in the business and financial communities. Nevertheless, businesses bite the bullet and implement the new rule, despite whatever objections they may have. Otherwise, their financial statements could be accused of being misleading because the company's accounting methods would not be in full compliance with GAAP.

Many FASB pronouncements deal with very technical accounting topics. The FASB has issued more than 150 pronouncements since it started in 1973. If you took the time to look over the list of all the pronouncements of the FASB (and its predecessors in accounting rule-making) I doubt if you would find many of general interest—although it should be said that corporate controllers, professional security analysts, and investment managers keep a close watch on all accounting rule changes.

Most of the FASB's pronouncements have registered less than a 3.0 on a financial statement Richter scale—they were barely noticed by investors and other financial statement users. On the other hand, certain FASB statements on accounting standards have caused severe earthquakes in financial state-ments and have been very controversial—involving bitter arguments and acrimonious accusations, to say nothing about intense lobbying of Congress and heavy-handed pressure on the FASB as well as assaults on its process. Accounting for management stock options is a good example of a controversial and very contentious issue facing the accounting profession, which we turn to next.

Stock Options: To Expense,
or Not to Expense?

One of the hottest accounting controversies today concerns *stock options*. Before delving into the thorny issue of accounting for stock options I first need to set the stage. So, please bear with me. An example helps explain things. I'll keep the example as simple and straightforward as possible.

For the year just ended suppose a business reports $10 million bottom-line net income. It has 10 million shares of capital stock outstanding (in the hands of its stockholders). Thus, its *earnings per share* (EPS) is $1.00. The market price of its shares equals 20 times its EPS, so the stock is selling at $20 per share. The ratio of market price to EPS is called the *price/earnings ratio*, a key ratio for investors that is discussed further in Chapter 22.

In the following scenarios assume that the price/earnings ratio remains constant at 20 times EPS. (Of course the ratio varies for most businesses over time, but holding it constant keeps things easier to follow and is not unrealistic.) The *market capitalization*, or *market cap*, of the business is therefore $200 million ($20 market price per share × 10 million shares = $200 million market cap).

In the fourth year following the year just ended, suppose the company earns $18 million bottom-line net income. Please reread the facts of the example, to have them firmly in mind as we look at the following scenarios.

Scenario #1—No New Stock Shares

Suppose the business does not issue any additional capital stock shares; four years later it still has 10 million shares of capital stock outstanding. So, its EPS is $1.80 ($18 million net income ÷ 10 million shares = $1.80 EPS). The market price of its stock shares is $36 ($1.80 EPS × 20 = $36). Its market cap has grown to $360 million ($36 per share × 10 million shares = $360 million market cap). Market cap jumped from $200 million to $360 million, for an $160 million increase over four years. The stockholders should be pleased.

Scenario #2—Additional Stock Shares

Suppose the company needed more capital to fuel its earnings growth. Therefore, the company issued 2 million additional shares to its stockholders at $20 per share for a total of $40 million. EPS for the fourth year is $1.50 ($18 million net income ÷ 12 million shares = $1.50 EPS). The stock price is $30 ($1.50 EPS × 20 = $30). The market cap is the same as in Scenario #1, or $360 million ($30 per share × 12 million shares = $360 million). The stockholders have done pretty well over the four years. Market cap increases $120 million over four years relative to their $240 million investment (the $200 million initial market cap plus the $40 million additional capital they invested in the business).

When a business corporation issues additional stock shares it generally has to give its present stockholders the right of first refusal to purchase the new shares, which is called the *preemptive right*. But there are exceptions to this general rule; stock options are one prominent exception. Before moving on to stock options, however, bear with me for one more scenario.

Scenario #3—Additional Stock Shares Purchased by New Stockholders

Suppose that the stockholders holding the 10 million shares decided not to purchase any of the additional capital stock shares. Therefore, the business issued 2 million additional shares to new stockholders. The original group would see their shares rise to $30, and the market cap of their shares would rise to $300 million ($30 market price × 10 million shares = $300 million market cap). The new group of stockholders would see the market cap of their shares grow from the $40 million they paid for the shares to $60 million (2 million shares × $30 market price per share = $60 million). The total market cap is still $360 million ($30 per share × 12 million shares = $360 million market cap).

The original stockholders left $20 million of market value appreciation on the table. If they had bought the additional shares for $40 million they would have realized $20 million market value increase on their $40 million investment. The original stockholders, by not purchasing the additional shares and instead allowing others to buy the shares, passed up $20 million in market value appreciation. The new stockholders who bought the additional capital stock shares realized the $20 million market value appreciation.

Scenario #4—Stock Options

Suppose the business, instead of offering the additional stock shares in the public market, grants several key managers options to purchase 2 million capital stock shares at $20 per share. The theory is that the managers will be better motivated to improve earnings and increase the market price of the company's stock. The managers exercised all their stock options and bought 2 million shares. Therefore, EPS in the fourth year is $1.50 ($18 million net income ÷ 12 million shares = $1.50 EPS). The stock's market price per share is $30 ($1.50 EPS × 20 = $30 per share).

The managers paid $40 million for their stock shares. Assume that they still own all the shares. Their shares are worth $60 million ($30 per share market value × 2 million shares = $60 million). The managers made a $20 million gain on their investment. Just as in Scenario #3, the $20 million gain by the managers came out of the pockets of the other stockholders. Presumably the other stockholders understand that allowing the managers to lock in a $20 per share price through their stock options gives away a good chunk of the market cap increase that otherwise would have gone to them.

Over the years stock options have became a larger and larger part of the typical management compensation package. So, the issue of whether the cost of stock options should be reported as an expense in the income statement has moved to the front burner. Currently the FASB is considering making mandatory the recording of stock option expense. As you might suspect, many businesses strongly oppose the recording of stock option expense.

The basic argument for *not* recording an expense is that stock options are a deal or an arrangement whereby the outside (non-management) stockholders knowingly agree to give up some of the market value appreciation of their shares that would accrue to them when earnings improve, in order to let managers have a share of the market value appreciation. There is no expense *to the business*, it is argued. True, there is an "expense," or "cost" to the nonmanagement stockholders. But it's not the job of accounting to keep track of the investment gains and losses among the stockholders of a business.

The basic argument for recording stock option expense is that everyone knows that these are a form of management compensation, and that all elements of management compensation should be recorded as expense. In other words, the bottom line should take into account the cost of stock options.

Stock option expense would be an unusual expense, to say the least. Instead of being recorded as a decrease in an asset or as an increase in a liability, as are all other expenses, the stock option expense would be recorded by an increase to owners' equity. In brief, net income would go down by recording the expense but in the same entry owners' equity is increased the same amount.

In my view the argument for recording stock option expense is motivated mainly by the desire to make the effects of stock options more transparent in the financial statements. A great deal of information is already presented in footnotes about a company's stock options. But many people think that footnote disclosure is not enough.

Some companies have voluntarily started to report stock option expense in their income statements. Most companies have not. No official poll has been taken, but my sense is that a sizable majority of businesses oppose expensing stock options. I doubt whether very many businesses will record stock option expense—unless forced to do so by the adoption of a new accounting standard.

As mentioned earlier, the accounting principles rule-making body (FASB) is seriously considering adopting such a rule. Many businesses are stepping up their lobbying with Congress to bring political pressure on the accounting profession to back off any accounting standard requiring the recording of stock option expense. Only time will tell how this plays out.

In closing I should mention that I have deliberately avoided many technical details of accounting for stock options as an expense. I doubt you're very interested in these complex problems. I'll just say that there are very serious technical problems in measuring the cost of stock options. If nothing else, it can be said with certainty that stock options have caused a lot of problems in the business and financial worlds—and not just accounting problems. Quite clearly, stock options were a major factor behind the many accounting fraud cases over recent years.

Finished and Unfinished Business

One main lesson from the history of the rule-making process over the years is that accounting rules, as good overall as they are today, have been slow in catching up with what's going on in the world of business. CPA auditors cannot force a business to use accounting methods that are different from GAAP. A CPA auditor could suggest to a business, "I think it would be better if you did it this way." But unless an accounting method is *required* under GAAP, auditors can only make suggestions.

Financial accounting does not have a built-in self-improvement process that would enable company accountants and CPA auditors to work together and improve accounting methods. Rather, everyone waits for the rule-making authority (FASB) to come out with new pronouncements on GAAP.

The FASB should be given a lot of credit for dealing with several contentious accounting problems over the three decades that it has served as the "supreme court" for setting financial reporting standards. It has issued accounting standards on the following vexing issues:

- *Financial derivatives*.
- Disclosure of *operating segments* of a business based on the company's organizational structure, and its *product groups*, *geographic areas*, and *major customers*.
- Disclosure about the *capital structure* of a business.
- Disclosure about *pension* and other *postretirement benefits* obligations of a business.

- Disclosure of *stock options* (although many think that the effect of these options should be recorded as an expense, which I discuss earlier in the chapter).

- *Impairment of assets*, which requires that a business write down any of its assets that will not contribute to the future revenue or income of the business.

- *Investments in securities*, and when to recognize gains and losses from these investments.

- *Statement of cash flows*, which was made a mandatory financial statement in 1987.

The FASB has also dealt with many industry-specific problems that needed attention, and it has issued many pronouncements on a variety of nagging accounting problems.

The FASB comes under much criticism, but no one has come up with a better alternative. The large majority of business managers, controllers, CPAs, lawyers, finance professionals, accounting professors, and financial institutions strongly favor keeping the role of setting financial accounting standards in the private sector and out of the hands of the federal government. I certainly agree. I also think that having the threat of the Securities and Exchange Commission (SEC) interceding in the process keeps the FASB on its toes and from going too much off the deep end.

Disclosure and Nondisclosure in Financial Reports

One criticism of the FASB's agenda over its three decades of existence has to do with disclosure in financial reports, or I should say the *lack of disclosure*. For example, I wish the FASB would give more attention to the potential *product liabilities* of businesses. Of more remote concern, though certainly on the horizon, are potential *environmental liabilities* of manufacturing companies, public utilities, and extractive industries.

For many years there have been persistent calls for more disclosure in financial reports. The central logic of the 1933 and 1934 federal securities laws is *full disclosure*. But several items of information—clearly of interest and relevance to investors, creditors, and other users of financial reports—are not required to be disclosed in external financial reports to stockholders.

Advertising and other marketing expenses do not have to be broken out separately in income statements, though they have to be reported in the annual 10-K filing with the Securities and Exchange Commission (SEC). Maintenance and repair expenses can be used to manipulate profit year to year (see Chapter 18, page 131). These expenses do not have to be reported in income statements, although they have to be disclosed in the annual 10-K with the SEC.

Compensation of top management does not have to be reported in a company's financial statements or in the footnotes. In contrast, this information must be disclosed in *proxy statements* of public corporations that are the means by which the boards of directors of corporations solicit the votes of stockholders. A summary schedule of who owns the stock shares of a corporation does not have to be—and hardly ever is—disclosed in financial reports.

Disclosure has improved over the years, to be sure. For example, a regular feature in financial reports today is the management discussion and analysis (MD&A) section, which explains the profit performance, problems, and strategy of the business. In my opinion, disclosure could be expanded still further without causing businesses any loss of their competitive advantages.

To be fair about this, I should mention that most organizations—religious, military, educational, other nonprofits, and governmental—are reluctant to make full disclosure of their financial affairs. Businesses are no exception to this general aversion to release too much information to the public.

The Securities and Exchange Commission (SEC) has established an electronic database for the financial statements and other filings by the public companies under its jurisdiction that is accessible over the Internet. This huge database of financial information is called the Electronic Data Gathering, Analysis, and Retrieval (EDGAR) system. Start at the SEC's web site (www.sec.gov) to navigate to the particular documents and information you want to find.

Most companies have made their financial reports available over the Internet. They have established web sites that provide a wide range of information. Several databases are available to search for information on specific companies.

In short, there are many different sources for digging up information about businesses. Their "hard copy" annual stockholders' financial reports will continue to be the centerpiece of information about profit performance, financial condition, and cash flow. Getting the information, on the other hand, will surely become more and more electronic in the future.

20

COST OF GOODS SOLD CONUNDRUM

Importance of This Accounting Choice

The cost of products sold to customers usually is a company's largest single expense, commonly being 50% to 70% of sales revenue. In contrast, many businesses sell *services* instead of products; examples are airlines, telephone companies, Disney World, and movie theaters. For product businesses, gross margin and all profit lines below gross margin depend on which accounting method is used to measure cost of goods sold expense.

Clearly managers have a stake in how profit is measured; so, they should understand how the biggest deduction against sales revenue is determined. In my view, the chief executive should decide which accounting method to use for the company's cost of goods sold expense. This decision also can have a major impact on the company's balance sheet, in particular its inventory asset account.

Three basic methods are widely used to determine cost of goods sold expense. All three methods have theoretical support. All three methods are accepted interpretations of the general accounting principle that the cost of products sold to customers should be matched against the revenue from the sales in order to correctly measure gross margin for the period. Putting cost of goods sold in one period and sales revenue of the goods sold in another period would make no sense at all.

Business managers and professional accountants disagree regarding exactly how to determine the cost of goods sold during the period. A specific example demonstrates the accounting problem and contrasts the differences among the three methods on gross margin and ending inventory cost.

Suppose a company sold 4,000 units of a product during the year just ended. (It doesn't make any difference whether the business manufactures the products it sells or is a retailer that purchases products for resale.) The company started the year with 1,000 units, which is the carryforward stock from last year.

Businesses do not let their inventory level drop to zero—unless a product is being phased out or because of circumstances beyond their control. So, the company in this example replaces products as they are sold during the year. The company replaced the 4,000 units sold and did not increase or decrease its inventory quantity during the year. Thus it ended the year with exactly the same number of units it started with, or 1,000 units.

The company made four acquisitions of products during the year, each being a batch of 1,000 units. The size of each batch manufactured or purchased may vary, of course; businesses do not necessarily acquire products in equal-size lots during the year. In summary, the company started the year with 1,000 units, sold 4,000 units, replaced the 4,000 units sold, and ended the year with 1,000 units.

If product costs never changed over time, there would be no

accounting problem. But, as you know, product costs fluctuate over time, and these cost changes cause an accounting problem that is solved in three different ways:

1. Average cost method.
2. Last-in, first-out (LIFO) method.
3. First-in, first-out (FIFO) method.

Exhibit 20.1 on this page presents the facts of the example. As you see, product cost drifted up over the year. Each successive acquisition cost the business $5,000 more than the one before. Before proceeding, I'd like your opinion on this accounting problem. How would you divide the $550,000 total cost between the 4,000 units sold and the 1,000 units on hand in inventory at year-end? (See Exhibit 20.1 again.) No fair sitting on the fence.

I believe that you would agree that the $550,000 total cost of the 5,000 units should be divided or allocated between cost of goods sold expense for the 4,000 units sold during the year and the inventory asset at year-end for the 1,000 units not yet sold. (These units will be sold and generate sales revenue next year.) You wouldn't charge the entire $550,000 of all 5,000 units against the sales revenue for only 4,000 units sold during the year, would you?

If you were the chief executive of this business, how would you divide the $550,000 total cost? Instead of making this decision yourself, you could let the company's controller make the decision. Too often managers simply sit on the sidelines and go along with the method recommended by their controllers. I think you should analyze the situation yourself and decide which is the best method for the business.

Like other management decisions, this one comes down to certain basic questions: What are the alternatives? What are the consequences of each alternative? Which alternative is best relative to the company's goals and strategy? If you were in a room with other business executives, I doubt that all of you would come to the same decision. The group probably would split into three camps on this question, which we turn to next.

EXHIBIT 20.1—COST OF GOODS SOLD EXPENSE AND ENDING INVENTORY COST EXAMPLE

Product Batches	Quantity	Cost
Beginning Inventory	1,000 units	$100,000
First Acquisition	1,000 units	105,000
Second Acquisition	1,000 units	110,000
Third Acquisition	1,000 units	115,000
Fourth Acquisition	1,000 units	120,000
Totals	5,000 units	$550,000
Goods Sold during Period	4,000 units	TBD*
Inventory at End of Period	1,000 units	TBD*

*TBD = to be determined by the choice of accounting method. See Exhibits 20.2, 20.3, and 20.4 for each of the three basic accounting methods.

Average Cost Method

Left on their own, without talking with their accountants, my guess is that most business managers would think that the *average cost method* would be the best way to deal with this problem. The average cost method is shown in Exhibit 20.2 on this page. The argument for this method is that four-fifths of the goods were sold, so four-fifths of the total cost should be charged to cost of goods sold expense and one-fifth should be allocated to the cost of ending inventory.

The logic is that gross margin (profit) is being measured for the *whole year*, so all costs for the year should be pooled and each unit should share and share alike—whether the unit was sold or not sold (still in ending inventory). Put another way, the average cost per unit is $110 ($550,000 total cost ÷ 5,000 total units = $110). This average cost is multiplied by the 4,000 units sold to calculate the $440,000 cost of goods sold expense. The ending inventory is $110,000, or 1,000 units in ending inventory times the $110 average cost per unit.

The average cost method has a lot of intuitive appeal and makes a lot of common sense. However, you might be surprised to learn that this method runs a distant third in popularity. Much more likely, a business would select one of the two other alternative accounting methods for determining cost of goods sold expense.

EXHIBIT 20.2—AVERAGE COST METHOD TO DETERMINE COST OF GOODS SOLD EXPENSE AND ENDING INVENTORY COST

Product Batches	Quantity	Cost
Beginning Inventory	1,000 units	$100,000
First Acquisition	1,000 units	105,000
Second Acquisition	1,000 units	110,000
Third Acquisition	1,000 units	115,000
Fourth Acquisition	1,000 units	120,000
Totals	5,000 units	$550,000
Goods Sold during Period	4,000 units	**$440,000**
Inventory at End of Period	1,000 units	**$110,000**

The $550,000 total cost is divided by the 5000 total units to calculate $110 average cost per unit. This $110 average cost is multiplied by 4,000 units sold to determine the $440,000 cost of goods sold expense, and by 1,000 units of ending inventory to determine the $110,000 cost for ending inventory.

Last-In, First-Out (LIFO) Method

The *last-in, first-out*, or LIFO method selects the four batches that were acquired during the year and charges the total of these four acquisitions to cost of goods sold expense. As you see in Exhibit 20.3 on this page, the total cost of the four batches is $450,000. The term "last-in" refers to the most recent, or latest acquisitions. The term "first-out" refers to charging the cost of a batch to expense before turning to the cost of another acquisition.

The primary theory for LIFO is that products sold have to be replaced to continue in business, and that the most recent (last-in) costs are nearest to the costs of replacing the products

sold. Acquisition costs increased during the year, so the LIFO method selects the batches with the highest costs. In periods of increasing costs LIFO maximizes the cost of goods sold expense.

The cost of the beginning inventory batch, $100,000 in this example, remains as the cost of ending inventory—as you see in Exhibit 20.3. The actual products on hand at year-end are not those at the start of the year, of course. The products on hand in ending inventory are from the most recent acquisition. The actual flow of products seldom follows a last-in, first-out sequence. The first products acquired usually are the first ones sold. No matter; LIFO ignores the actual physical flow of products. LIFO takes the most recent (last-in) batches for determining cost of goods sold expense for the year.

As a result, LIFO leaves in ending inventory the residual cost of products after selecting the most recent batches for cost of goods sold. The LIFO method leaves the *oldest* cost in inventory. After several years of using LIFO a company's inventory reminds me of the story of Dorian Gray looking in the mirror. The actual inventory is young, but its reported cost in the balance sheet is old, perhaps very old. Please refer again to Caterpillar's footnote on page 104; its LIFO inventory is about $2 billion below the current cost of the inventory because the company has used LIFO for many years.

When there is steady cost inflation (as in this example) LIFO maximizes cost of goods sold expense, and thus minimizes profit

EXHIBIT 20.3—LIFO METHOD TO DETERMINE COST OF GOODS SOLD EXPENSE AND ENDING INVENTORY COST

Product Batches	Quantity	Cost
Beginning Inventory	1,000 units	$100,000
First Acquisition	1,000 units	105,000
Second Acquisition	1,000 units	110,000
Third Acquisition	1,000 units	115,000
Fourth Acquisition	1,000 units	120,000
Totals	5,000 units	$550,000
Goods Sold during Period	4,000 units	450,000
Inventory at End of Period	1,000 units	$100,000

(or, I should say, gross margin). The side effect of doing this, however, is that inventory in the balance sheet is reported at the oldest, or lowest, cost.

LIFO produces predictable effects when product costs steadily increase year to year—that is, cost of goods sold expense is maximized and inventory cost gets older and older. Keep in mind, however, that this is only one of several different scenarios. The manufacturing costs of some products actually decline over the years. Some products have very short life cycles—new models replace the old models every year or so. Therefore, inventory cost does not have time enough to get very old. And if product costs remain stable and don't change very much over time, the choice of accounting method makes little difference.

The First-In, First-Out (FIFO) Method

The LIFO method selects costs in *reverse* chronological order. In contrast, the *first-in*, *first-out* (FIFO) method takes costs in chronological order for determining cost of goods sold expense. The FIFO method in this example selects the beginning inventory batch and the first, second, and third acquisition batches to make up the total cost for the 4,000 units sold during the year. The sum of these four batches is $430,000—see Exhibit 20.4 on this page. The first batches of products acquired are the first to be charged out to cost of goods sold expense. The cost of the most recent batch remains as the cost of ending inventory.

One reason for using FIFO is that the actual flow of products in most situations follows a first-in, first-out sequence. In periods of cost inflation, as in this example, FIFO minimizes the cost of goods sold expense and maximizes gross margin. And ending inventory is reported at the most recent, or highest, cost in the balance sheet.

The strongest reason for adopting FIFO is when a business sets its sales prices according to a FIFO-based method, which is discussed later in the chapter. First we look at the differences among the three methods.

EXHIBIT 20.4—FIFO METHOD TO DETERMINE COST OF GOODS SOLD EXPENSE AND ENDING INVENTORY COST

Product Batches	Quantity	Cost
Beginning Inventory	1,000 units	$100,000
First Acquisition	1,000 units	105,000
Second Acquisition	1,000 units	110,000
Third Acquisition	1,000 units	115,000
Fourth Acquisition	1,000 units	120,000
Totals	5,000 units	$550,000
Goods Sold during Period	4,000 units	**$430,000**
Inventory at End of Period	1,000 units	**$120,000**

So, Which Method to Use?

Suppose you're the chief executive of the business in this example. At year-end you review the profit performance of every product the business sells. The sales revenue from the 4,000 units of product sold is $645,000 for the year. How much gross margin did you earn on this product for the year? The answer depends on which accounting method you decide to use.

The gross margins for each accounting method would be as follows:

Average Cost Method
Sales Revenue	$645,000
Cost of Goods Sold Expense (Exhibit 20.2)	440,000
Gross Margin	$205,000

LIFO Method
Sales Revenue	$645,000
Cost of Goods Sold Expense (Exhibit 20.3)	450,000
Gross Margin	$195,000

FIFO Method
Sales Revenue	$645,000
Cost of Goods Sold Expense (Exhibit 20.4)	430,000
Gross Margin	$215,000

Sales revenue is the same; the business set its sales prices and sold 4,000 units, which generated $645,000 sales reve-

nue for the year. Only the cost of goods sold expense amounts differ.

The merits of each accounting method can be debated until the cows come home. Personally, I think the proper method is the one that is most consistent with the *sales pricing policy and strategy* of the business. In other words, I need to know how a business goes about setting sales prices before I can decide on the proper cost of goods sold expense accounting method for the business.

Suppose that a business sets its sales prices as follows. It starts with the cost of manufacture or purchase of a batch of products. The company marks up the cost per unit to set the sales price. It holds to this sales price until all units are sold from the batch, and then moves on to the next batch and repeats the process. Many factors other than product cost affect sales prices, of course. Absent other pressures on sales prices, many companies set their target sales prices in this manner, although these benchmark sales prices may be just the point of departure. A business may increase or lower its final sales prices because of competition and other economic pressures.

For the product in this example, suppose the company uses a first-in, first-out sales pricing approach; it marks up product cost 50% to set sales prices and was able to sell the product at these sales prices. Therefore, the company's sales revenue for the year for this product was determined as follows (see Exhibit 20.1 on page 149):

50% Markup on Cost to Set Sales Prices

$100,000 × 150% = $150,000
$105,000 × 150% = $157,500
$110,000 × 150% = $165,000
$115,000 × 150% = $172,500

Total Sales Revenue = $645,000

If the business sets sales prices in this manner, I definitely favor the FIFO cost of goods sold expense method. Gross margin equals exactly one-third of sales revenue: ($215,000 gross margin ÷ $645,000 sales revenue = ⅓ exactly). Both the average cost method and LIFO would give a gross margin ratio lower than one-third, which is inconsistent with the company's sales pricing method.

Regardless of how they set sales prices, many businesses adopt the LIFO method—despite the fact that this method yields the lowest gross margin and the lowest ending inventory cost in periods of rising costs. One possible reason is conservatism. Many companies, it seems, prefer to err on the downside and not be accused of overstating profits and assets.

Another possible reason for LIFO could be to minimize the amount that is subject to a profit-sharing or profit-based bonus plan—although employees and managers wouldn't like this, of course. Still another reason might be to hide profit during periods of labor problems or union contract bargaining. Perhaps a business wants to appear to be in need of more profit and thus be justified to raise its sales prices or to lay off employees.

Or the main reason may be simply to minimize *taxable income*. LIFO is allowed for federal income tax purposes. LIFO reduces taxable income by $20,000 compared with FIFO in this example. However, if income tax rates are forecast to go up in the near future it might be better to use FIFO and report higher taxable income this year while tax rates are lower than they will be in the future.

Cash flow is also very important. A business could be in a very tight cash position and need to hang on to every dollar of cash for as long as possible. So, the company could elect LIFO to delay paying income tax. Even if not strapped for cash, a business can invest the temporary tax savings from using LIFO and earn a return on the investment. If inflation is forecast to continue in the future, then a business could delay paying its income taxes as long as possible and pay in the cheaper dollars of the future.

Odds and Ends

Two inventory and cost of goods sold expense accounting topics are discussed briefly in this final section of the chapter:

1. LIFO liquidation gains.

2. Lower of cost or market write-downs of inventory.

The first is a unique feature of the LIFO method. The second applies to all businesses, no matter which accounting method they use.

LIFO Liquidation Gains

When deciding whether to use the LIFO method, business managers should think ahead about what could happen at the end of a product's life cycle. In the terminal year there could be a *LIFO liquidation gain* caused by reducing inventory to zero.

Please refer again to Exhibit 20.3 on page 151, which shows the LIFO method for the example. Fast-forward five years into the future; assume the product reaches the end of its life cycle and is phased out early in the year. The company maintains its inventory level at 1,000 units. Therefore, the company sells the last 1,000 units of this product. These 1,000 units are on the books at $100,000. Every year the business replaced the units sold and the cost of these replacement units were charged to the cost of goods sold expense. Thus, the inventory remained at $100,000 cost over

the years. The most recent batch of 1,000 units of this product cost $220,000 (product cost continued to increase over the years).

The business sold the 1,000 remaining units of this product early in the year. Because the product was being discontinued, the business dropped the sales price. To move the product out the door the business sold the 1,000 units for $220,000 sales revenue, which was the cost of the most recent acquisition. The cost of the most recent acquisition had already been charged to cost of goods sold expense—this is how LIFO works (see Exhibit 20.3 on page 151). The only cost available for the final 1,000 units sold is the old cost—the $100,000 amount from five years ago.

Compared with the most recent $220,000 acquisition cost, there would be zero gross margin on the final sales. However, the final sale results in recording gross margin of $120,000 ($220,000 sales revenue minus $100,000 old cost of inventory sold = $120,000 gross margin). This onetime nonrecurring effect is called a *LIFO liquidation gain*. Taxable income is also $120,000 higher as a result of phasing out the product.

The lesson to be learned from this example is that by using the LIFO method, a business simply defers or delays recording a certain amount of gross margin—both in its annual income statements and in its annual income tax returns. Eventually, when the business reaches the end of a product's life cycle and liquidates the inventory of the product, the gross margin that would have been recorded along the way under the FIFO or average cost method catches up with the business and has to be recorded.

Managers should be aware of the eventual LIFO liquidation gain that probably will happen at the end of a product's life cycle.

To go a step further on this point, a business manager does not have to wait until the end of a product's life cycle to record this gain. Instead, a manager could force this effect by deliberately allowing LIFO-based inventory to fall below normal levels. How? Toward the end of the year the manager could hold off making acquisitions, thus causing inventory quantity to drop to abnormally low levels.

Inventory levels may drop below normal levels for other reasons. For instance, a prolonged labor strike may force a business to drastically reduce its inventory levels. Whatever the reasons, when ending inventory is below the inventory quantities on hand at the start of the year, a business has to dip into its old LIFO cost layers, which produces a LIFO liquidation gain effect.

In summary, businesses that use LIFO have some profit (gross margin) in reserve or "on the shelf" that is ready to be recorded at any time, assuming product cost has drifted up over the years. There is nothing to prohibit a business from manipulating profit by the partial liquidation of its LIFO-based inventory. If material in amount, a LIFO liquidation gain (being nonrecurring in nature) should be disclosed in a footnote to the financial statements, or as extraordinary income in its income statement for the period.

Lower of Cost or Market (LCM)

Regardless of which accounting method a business uses—average cost, FIFO, or LIFO—at the end of each year the company compares the sales value and replacement cost value of all products in its ending inventory with their recorded cost. If market value (what a product can be sold for or what a product could be replaced for at that time) is lower than the recorded cost of the product, then the product's cost is written down to the lower amount. This procedure is called *lower of cost or market* (LCM), or "cost or market, whichever is lower."

The purpose of writing down inventory cost is to recognize any loss in sales value of products and to recognize that the cost of replacing the products may have fallen below the recorded cost of the products. Please refer to Exhibit 20.4 for the FIFO method (page 153). The units in ending inventory are carried on the books at $120,000. Assume that, quite unexpectedly, demand for the product took a nosedive just before year-end. The business reduced the sales price drastically to move these units out the door. In this situation the business would write down the cost of the products. The amount of the write-down is recorded as an expense in the period.

21

DEPRECIATION DILEMMAS

Depreciation Foibles

A basic principle of financial accounting is that the cost of the long-term operating resources used by a business should be allocated over the years these fixed assets are used. It is definitely against generally accepted accounting principles (GAAP) to charge the entire cost of such an asset to expense in the year of its purchase or construction. The allocation of cost over a fixed asset's useful life is called *depreciation*.

Chapter 9 introduces depreciation accounting and the *accumulated depreciation* account; the balance of this contra account is deducted from the cost of fixed assets in the balance sheet. The *book value* of fixed assets equals their original cost less the accumulated depreciation on these long-term operating resources. This chapter discusses practical problems of depreciation accounting. Instead of the theoretically correct method, often a business takes shortcuts to deal with the problems in the most expedient manner.

In reading this chapter please keep in mind the cash flow aspects of depreciation. Chapter 13 explains that depreciation is one of the key adjustments to net income for determining cash flow from profit (or to be technically correct, cash flow from operating activities). Sales revenue each year, in part, recovers some of the original capital invested in fixed assets. In rough terms the depreciation recapture can be compared with taking money out each year from a savings account (capital invested in fixed assets) and putting the money in a checking account.

Fixed assets are long-term capital investments by a business.

Over the years of their use the company has to recover through sales revenue the amount of capital invested in these assets. A business does not hold fixed assets for the purpose of selling them sometime in the future for more than it paid for them. At the end of their useful lives fixed assets are sent to the junk pile or sold for their salvage value. Well, this is generally true, *except for land and buildings*.

Machinery, equipment, tools, and vehicles do not appreciate in value over the years of their use. The clock is ticking on the usefulness of these fixed assets. However, land and buildings are a different kettle of fish. The cost of land is not depreciated. The cost of buildings is depreciated, even though the market value of the buildings may appreciate over time. It can be argued that the cost of buildings should not be depreciated when their market value holds steady or increases. But GAAP says to depreciate the cost of buildings, no matter what. This is the first thing to keep in mind about depreciation. The next thing to keep in mind is best explained with an example.

Suppose a business buys several new delivery trucks. The total purchase invoice cost paid to the dealer for the fleet of trucks is *capitalized* (i.e., recorded as an increase in the fixed asset account for these operating resources that will be used over several years). The term capitalized comes from the idea of making a capital investment. The amount of sales taxes paid by the business is also capitalized; sales taxes are a direct and inseparable add-on cost of the trucks. So far there is no argument; both the total purchase invoice cost and sales taxes paid by the buyer are capitalized. Beyond these two direct costs accounting theory and actual accounting practice part company.

Suppose the business paints its new trucks with the company's name, address, telephone number, and logo. Also, the business installs special racks and fittings in the trucks. In theory these additional costs should be capitalized and included in the cost basis of the fixed assets. These additional costs are not directly part of the purchase; these costs are detachable and separate from the purchase cost. Nevertheless, the costs should be capitalized because the costs improve the value in use of the trucks.

When purchasing many long-lived operating assets, a business incurs additional costs that should be added to the cost basis, but in fact may not be. Accounting theory says to capitalize these costs. As a practical matter, however, only purchase cost plus other direct costs of purchase are capitalized. Any additional costs are recorded as expenses immediately, instead of being depreciated over the useful lives of the fixed assets.

There are countless examples of such additional costs. A business may paint several signs on a new building it just moved into. It may fumigate the entire building before moving in. It may upgrade the lighting in several areas. After purchasing new machines or new equipment a business usually incurs costs of installing the assets and preparing them for use. Such additional costs should be capitalized, according to accounting theory.

In actual practice, however, the additional costs are usually not recorded in a company's fixed assets. Instead the costs are charged to expense in the period incurred. One reason is to deduct these costs immediately for income tax purposes—to minimize current taxable income in the year the costs are incurred. (A business should be very careful regarding what the Internal Revenue Service tolerates in this regard.) Another reason for not capitalizing such costs is simply that of practical expediency. It is much easier to charge such costs to expense rather than adding them to the fixed asset cost.

While on the topic of practical expediency I should mention that most businesses buy an assortment of relatively low-cost tools and equipment items—examples are hammers, power saws, drills, floor-cleaning machines, dollies, pencil sharpeners, lamps, and so on. The costs of these assets, since they will be used several years, should be capitalized and depreciated over their expected useful lives. Keeping a separate depreciation schedule for each screwdriver or pencil sharpener is ridiculous, of course.

Most businesses set minimum dollar limits below which costs of fixed assets are not capitalized but are charged directly to expense. This is accepted practice; CPA auditors tolerate this practice as long as a business is consistent one year to the next. The only question concerns the *materiality* of such costs. If these costs in the aggregate were extraordinarily high one year, the CPA auditors, as well as the Internal Revenue Service, might object.

In any case, business managers should understand the financial statement effects of not capitalizing additional costs associated with buying fixed assets and not capitalizing the costs of small tools and equipment. To illustrate, suppose a business purchased new fixed assets during the year. The sum of the invoice prices plus sales taxes for all these assets was $1,400,000 for the year. The $1,400,000 is capitalized; the business records this cost in its fixed asset accounts. If it didn't, the company's CPA auditors would object in the strongest possible terms, and the IRS could accuse the business of income tax evasion (which is a felony).

In addition to the direct costs of the new fixed assets, suppose the business spent $120,000 during the year for the types of additional costs connected with buying new fixed assets that were just described, and spent another $20,000 for small tools and inexpensive equipment items. The $140,000 total could have been properly capitalized, but consistent with previous years the company records the amount to expense.

To simplify, assume that the various fixed assets are depreciated over seven years, and that the business uses the straight-line depreciation method. (As will be discussed shortly, many businesses use an accelerated depreciation method instead of the straight-line method.) The effects of capitalizing only the direct costs versus capitalizing all costs are compared:

Annual Expenses If Only Direct Acquisition Costs Are Capitalized

Year 1: $200,000 depreciation + $140,000	$340,000
Years 2–7: $1,400,000 ÷ 7 years	$200,000

Annual Expenses If All Costs Are Capitalized

Years 1–7: $1,540,000 ÷ 7 years	~ $220,000

If the business chooses the first alternative, then expenses in the first year are $120,000 higher ($340,000 minus $220,000 = $120,000). But then annual depreciation expense is $20,000 less for the next six years. If all costs are capitalized, every year is treated equally. Total expenses over the entire seven years are the same either way. It's year by year that expenses are different.

One word of caution: This comparison does not consider the carryover effects from previous years. We would have to know the history of the business regarding these costs in previous years to determine the final *net* effect on this year.

Chapter 18 discusses massaging the accounting numbers to control the amount of profit (net income) recorded in the year. Charging the costs of small tools and equipment items to expense provides business managers yet another way to manipulate profit for the year. The timing of these expenditures is discretionary. Small tools can be replaced before the end of the year or put off until next year. So the expense can be recorded this year or delayed until next year.

To Accelerate or Not?

Most business buildings last 50, 75, or more years. Yet under the federal income tax law the cost of nonresidential buildings used by a business can be depreciated over 39 years. Most autos and light trucks used by businesses last 10 years or longer, but can be depreciated over 5 years under the tax law.

In brief, the federal income tax law permits business fixed assets to be depreciated over a shorter number of years than the actual useful lives of the assets. This is the deliberate economic policy of Congress to encourage capital investment in newer, technologically superior resources to help improve the productivity of American business.

Accelerated depreciation deductions are higher and tax payments are lower in the early years of using fixed assets. Thus, the business has more cash flow available to reinvest in new fixed assets—both to expand capacity and to improve productivity. This *accelerated depreciation* philosophy has become a permanent feature of the income tax law, and is not likely to change anytime soon.

The federal income tax law regarding depreciation of fixed assets has effectively discouraged any realistic attempt at estimating the useful lives of a company's long-lived operating resources. This is a fact of business life, like it or not. The shortest lives permitted for income tax are selected by most (but not all) businesses for reporting depreciation expense in their financial statements. The schedules of these short, or accelerated, useful lives are found in the section of the income tax law named the "Modified Accelerated Cost Recovery System" (MACRS).

Alternatively, the income tax code permits businesses to adopt longer useful life estimates than the MACRS schedules. But even these longer lives are generally shorter than realistic forecasts of the actual useful lives of most business fixed assets.

MACRS also allows the front-end loading of depreciation, instead of a level and equal amount of depreciation each year (called the *straight-line* method). More depreciation is allocated to the early years and less in the later years. The annual depreciation amounts "walk down the stairs," each year being less than the year before. Like the LIFO accounting method for cost of goods sold expense, I seriously doubt whether accelerated depreciation would be used by many businesses if this method were not allowed for income tax.

Financial statement users should keep in mind that, with some exceptions, business fixed assets are overdepreciated—not in the actual wearing out or physical using up sense but in the accounting sense. In balance sheets the reported book values of a company's fixed assets (original cost less accumulated depreciation) are understated. A company's fixed assets are written off too fast. Book values shrink much quicker than they should.

In summary, a business has two basic alternatives regarding how to record depreciation expense on its fixed assets:

1. Adopt the *accelerated income tax approach*—use the shortest useful lives and the front-end loaded depreciation allocation allowed by the tax code.

2. Adopt more realistic (longer) useful life estimates for fixed assets and allocate the cost in equal amounts to each year—*straight-line depreciation*.

For an example, assume that a business pays $120,000 for a new machine. Under MACRS this asset falls in the 7-year class. Alternatively, the business could elect to use a 12-year useful life estimate, which we'll assume to be realistic for this particular machine.

Exhibit 21.1 (page 165) compares the annual depreciation amounts determined by the double-declining accelerated depreciation schedule permitted by MACRS with the $10,000 annual depreciation amount according to the straight-line method. (Generally only one-half year depreciation can be deducted in the year of acquisition under the income tax law.)

Suppose the machine actually is used for 12 years. Therefore, this asset adds value to the operations of the business every year of its use. The value added in some years may be more than in other years. It's virtually impossible to determine exactly how much sales revenue any one machine is responsible for—or any particular fixed asset, for that matter. Nevertheless, it bothers me that if the business chooses accelerated depreciation, then the last five years of using the machine would not be charged with any depreciation expense. What do you think?

Although accelerated depreciation has obvious income tax advantages, there are certain disadvantages. For one thing, the book (reported) values of a company's long-term operating assets are lower. When loaning money a lender looks at the company's assets as reported in its balance sheet. The lower book values of fixed assets caused by using accelerated depreciation may, in effect, lower the debt capacity of a business (the maximum amount it could borrow).

One final point: Managers and investors are very interested in whether a business was able to improve its profit performance over the previous year. Ideally, when a profit increase is reported in an income statement, the increase should be due to real causes—better profit margins on sales, gains in operating efficiency, higher sales volumes, and so forth.

Spurious increases in profit can be misleading. Profit trends are difficult to track if there are drop-offs in annual depreciation expense, which happens under accelerated depreciation (see Exhibit 21.1 again). The straight-line method has one advantage: Depreciation expense is constant year to year on the same fixed assets.

EXHIBIT 21.1—COMPARISON OF DEPRECIATION METHODS

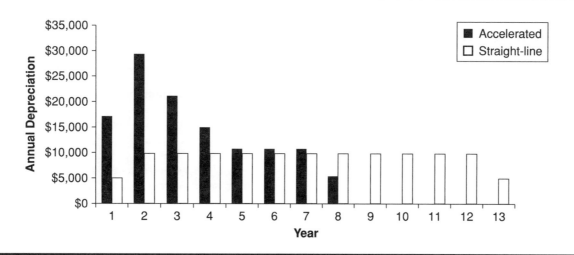

A Quick Word on Amortization

Spreading the cost of a long-term *intangible* asset to expense over its predicted economic life is called *amortization*. Chapter 9 introduces this expense, which is of the same nature as depreciation expense. Amortization refers to intangible assets; depreciation refers to tangible assets. Only the straight-line allocation method is used for recording amortization expense. Accelerated (front-end loaded) allocation methods are not used.

There are no generally accepted schedules of useful lives for amortizing intangible assets. Each intangible asset is relatively unique. At one time useful life estimates for recording amortization expense could not be longer than 40 years. Recently, however, this rule was relaxed. Businesses now do not have to record amortization expense on those intangibles it judges to have perpetual usefulness to the business. However, many businesses adopt life estimates 15 years or shorter for their intangible assets. The useful life periods being used by a business for recording amortization expense are disclosed in the footnotes to its financial statements.

In their balance sheets some businesses disclose both the cost of their intangible assets and the amount of accumulated amortization, which is deducted from cost. Alternatively, businesses may report their intangible assets *net* of accumulated amortization, which is permitted by generally accepted accounting principles. Both cost and accumulated depreciation should be presented for a company's tangible fixed assets.

Occasionally businesses record large write-downs on some of their tangible assets because they have become *impaired* (have lost part or all of their value). You see these extraordinary losses in income statements more often that you might expect. Fixed asset write-downs typically are recorded when a business is going through a major restructuring of the organization, or is downsizing its scale of operations. Write-downs of intangible assets are not necessarily associated with a restructuring or downsizing of the business.

A business should explain in a footnote why it decided to write down its intangible assets. The basic reason is that the business came to the conclusion that certain of its intangible assets are not worth what it paid for the assets. The business has egg on its face in making writedowns of its intangible assets. On the other hand, once written down no amortization expense is recorded in future periods on the amount of the write-down. The decks of future income statements are cleared of this amount of expense.

22

RATIOS FOR CREDITORS AND INVESTORS

The Purpose of Financial Statements

The twofold purpose of externally reported financial statements is to provide useful financial information about a business to its investors and lenders and to render an accounting to its sources of capital. Others may be interested in the financial affairs of a business—for example, its employees and other creditors. The primary audience of financial statements is the owner-investors in a business and its lenders. Financial reporting standards and generally accepted accounting principles (GAAP) have been developed with this primary audience in mind.

The dissemination of financial information by publicly owned businesses, those whose capital stock shares and other securities are traded in public markets, is governed by federal law, which is enforced mainly by the Securities and Exchange Commission (SEC). The New York Stock Exchange, Nasdaq, and other securities markets also enforce many rules and regulations regarding the release and communication of financial information by companies whose securities are traded on their markets.

For instance, a business cannot selectively release information to some stockholders or lenders but not to others, nor can a business tip off some of them before informing the others. The laws and accepted practices of financial reporting are designed to ensure that all stockholders and lenders have equal access to a company's financial information and financial statements.

A company's financial statements may not be the first source of information about its profit performance. Public corporations put out press releases consisting of short summaries of their most recent earnings results. These press releases precede mailing the company's latest financial report to its stockholders and lenders. Privately owned or nonpublic businesses do not usually send out letters to their owners and lenders in advance of their financial statements, although they could, of course.

This chapter examines what stockholders and lenders do with the financial statements once they get them. The chapter centers on the annual set of financial statements, which is the most complete. (Quarterly financial reports are abbreviated versions of the annual reports.) In particular, this chapter focuses on certain *ratios* that are useful to take the measure of a company's situation and achievements, and to pinpoint potential trouble spots.

Overview of Financial Statements

A company's financial statements are reproduced in Exhibit 22.1 on page 170. This is the same company example used in earlier chapters. The footnotes for these statements are not presented. (Chapter 16 discusses footnotes to financial statements.)

The company in this example is privately owned, which means its capital stock shares are not traded in a public market. The business has about 50 shareholders; a few of them are executives of the business, including the CEO, president, vice presidents, and other top-level managers. A business this size could go into the public marketplace for equity capital through an initial public offering (IPO) of capital stock shares and become publicly owned.

The chapter does not pretend to cover the broad field of *securities analysis* (i.e., the analysis of stocks and debt instruments issued by corporations). This broad field includes the analysis of competitive advantages and disadvantages of a business, domestic and international economic developments, business combination possibilities, and much more. The key ratios explained in the chapter are basic building blocks in securities analysis.

Also, the chapter does not discuss the important topic of trend analysis, which involves comparing a company's latest financial statements with its previous years' statements to identify important year-to-year changes. For example, investors and lenders are very interested in the sales growth or decline of a business, and the resulting impact on profit performance, cash flow, and financial condition.

The chapter has a more modest objective—to explain basic ratios used in financial statement analysis. Only a handful of ratios are discussed in the chapter, but they are extremely important and widely used.

Upon opening a company's financial report probably one of the first things most investors do is to give the financial statements a once-over; they do a fairly quick scan of the financial statements, in other words. What do they look for? In my experience, they look first at the bottom line of the income statement, to see if the business made a profit or suffered a loss for the year.

As one sports celebrity put it when explaining how he keeps tabs on his various business investments, he looks first to see if the bottom line has "parentheses around it." The business in our example does not; it avoided a loss. Its income statement reports that the business earned $2,642,000 net income for the year. Is this profit performance good, mediocre, or poor? Ratios help answer this question.

This company does not report any *extraordinary gains or losses* for the year, which are onetime, nonrecurring events. For example, a business may sell a major fixed asset and record a gain. Or a business may record a restructuring charge for the cost of laying off employees who will receive severance packages. These nonordinary, unusual gains and losses are reported separately from the ongoing, continuing operations of a company. This topic would lead into a labyrinth of technical details. But be warned: These irregular

EXHIBIT 22.1—EXTERNAL FINANCIAL STATEMENTS OF BUSINESS (without footnotes)

Dollar Amounts in Thousands, Except Earnings per Share

INCOME STATEMENT FOR YEAR

Sales Revenue	$52,000
Cost of Goods Sold	33,800
Gross Margin	$18,200
Operating Expenses	12,480
Depreciation Expense	785
Amortization Expense	325
Operating Earnings	$ 4,610
Interest Expense	545
Earnings before Tax	$ 4,065
Income Tax Expense	1,423
Net Income	$ 2,642
Basic Earnings per Share	$3.30

STATEMENT OF CHANGES IN STOCKHOLDERS' EQUITY

	Capital Stock	Retained Earnings
Beginning Balances	$7,950	$13,108
Net Income for Year		2,642
Shares Issued during Year	175	
Dividends Paid during Year		(750)
Ending Balances	$8,125	$15,000

BALANCE SHEET AT END OF YEAR

Assets

Cash	$ 3,265
Accounts Receivable	5,000
Inventory	8,450
Prepaid Expenses	960
Total Current Assets	$17,675
Property, Plant, and Equipment	16,500
Accumulated Depreciation	(4,250)
Goodwill	7,850
Accumulated Amortization	(2,275)
Total Assets	$35,500

Liabilities and Owners' Equity

Accounts Payable	$ 3,320
Accrued Expenses	1,515
Income Tax Payable	165
Short-Term Notes Payable	3,125
Total Current Liabilities	$ 8,125
Long-Term Notes Payable	4,250
Total Liabilities	$12,375
Stockholders' Equity:	
Capital Stock (800,400 shares)	8,125
Retained Earnings	15,000
Total Owners' Equity	$23,125
Total Liabilities and Owners' Equity	$35,500

STATEMENT OF CASH FLOWS FOR YEAR

Net Income—See Income Statement	$2,642
Accounts Receivable Increase	(320)
Inventory Increase	(935)
Prepaid Expenses Increase	(275)
Depreciation Expense	785
Amortization Expense	325
Accounts Payable Increase	645
Accrued Expenses Increase	480
Income Tax Payable Increase	83
Cash Flow from Operating Activities	$ 3,430
Purchases of Property, Plant, and Equipment	$(3,050)
Purchase of Goodwill	(900)
Cash Flow from Investing Activities	(3,950)
Increase in Short-Term Notes Payable	$ 125
Increase in Long-Term Notes Payable	500
Issue of Additional Capital Stock Shares	175
Cash Dividends Paid Shareholders	(750)
Cash Flow from Financing Activities	50
Decrease in Cash during Year	$ (470)

gains and losses complicate the evaluation and forecasting of the profit performance!

After reading the income statement, most financial statement readers probably take a quick look at the company's assets and compare them with the liabilities of the business. Are the assets adequate to the demands of the company's liabilities? Ratios help answer this question. Next, the readers take a look at the company's cash flows. As you see, the company's statement of cash flows is included in Exhibit 22.1. This is one of the primary financial statements of a business entity that must be included in its external financial reports. Nevertheless, I almost did *not* include it in the exhibit, which might surprise you.

None of the ratios discussed in this chapter involve the cash flow statement. Investors and creditors have yet to develop any benchmark ratios for cash flows. Still, cash flow gets a lot of ink in the financial press and in reports on corporations published by brokers and investment advisors. Cash flow from profit (operating activities) is considered a key variable for a business. The business in our example realized $3,430,000 cash flow from profit for the year just ended, which is less than its $3,950,000 capital expenditures for the year. Its other sources and uses of cash provided only $50,000 cash for the year. Thus, the company's cash balance dropped $470,000 during the year.

Reading the cash flow statement in this manner provides a useful synopsis of where the business got its money during the year and what it did with the money. Notice that no ratios were calculated. We could divide cash flow from profit by net income to determine cash flow as a percent of net income. I think this is an interesting ratio. But it is not one of the benchmark ratios used in financial statement analysis.

We could divide cash flow from profit (operating activities) by the number of capital stock shares to get cash flow per share. But the Financial Accounting Standards Board (FASB) has specifically discouraged this ratio, which is most unusual. It is quite rare for the FASB to go out of its way to put the kibosh on a particular ratio.

Exhibit 22.1 introduces a new financial statement—the *Statement of Changes in Stockholders' Equity*. In some respects this is not really a financial statement; it's more of a supporting schedule that summarizes changes in the capital stock and retained earnings accounts. The business in our example probably would include this statement. However, this schedule is not all that necessary because the changes in its two stockholder equity accounts are easy to follow.

The business issued additional shares of capital stock during the year, as reported in its statement of cash flows. So, the balance in its capital stock account increased. Net income for the year increased retained earnings, and the cash dividends paid to stockholders decreased the account.

The statement of changes in stockholders' equity is definitely needed when a business has a complex capitalization (ownership) structure that includes different classes of stock, and when a business repurchased some of its own capital stock shares during the year. Also, certain types of losses and gains are recorded directly to retained earnings and thus bypass the income statement. In these situations the statement of changes in stockholders' equity is essential to organize and report everything in one place.

Debt-Paying Ability, Liquidity, and Solvency Ratios

Stock analysts, investment portfolio managers, individual investors, investment bankers, economists, and others are interested in three key financial aspects of a business—cash flows, solvency, and profit performance. Cash flow analysis does not use ratios (at least not yet). In contrast, the analysis of solvency and profit performance makes use of several benchmark ratios.

Bankers and other lenders when deciding whether to make and renew loans to a business direct their attention to certain key financial statement ratios. These ratios provide a useful financial profile of the business for assessing its creditworthiness and for judging the ability of the business to pay its loans and interest on time.

Solvency refers to the ability of a business to pay its liabilities when they come due. Maintaining solvency (debt-paying ability) is essential for every business. If a business defaults on its debt obligations it becomes vulnerable to legal proceedings that could stop the company in its tracks, or at least could interfere with its normal operations.

Note: From here forward in the chapter all dollar amounts from the financial statements are in thousands (as they are in the financial statements).

The Current Ratio: Test of Short-Term Solvency

The *current ratio* is used to test the short-term liability-paying ability of a business. It's calculated by dividing total current assets by total current liabilities in a company's most recent balance sheet. From the data in Exhibit 22.1, the current ratio for the company is computed as follows:

$$\frac{\$17,675 \text{ Current Assets}}{\$8,125 \text{ Current Liabilities}} = 2.18 \text{ Current Ratio}$$

The current ratio is hardly ever expressed as a percent (which would be 218% in this case). The current ratio is stated as 2.18 to 1.00 for this company, or more simply just as 2.18.

The general rule, or standard, is that the current ratio for a business should be 2 to 1 or higher. Most businesses find that this minimum current ratio is expected by their creditors. In other words, short-term creditors generally like to see a business limit its current liabilities to one-half or less of its current assets.

Why do short-term creditors put this limit on a business? The main reason is to provide a safety cushion of protection for the payment of its short-term liabilities. A current ratio of 2 to 1 means there is $2 of cash or assets that should be converted into cash during the near future that will be available to pay each $1 of current liabilities that come due in roughly the same time period. Each dollar of short-term liabilities is backed up with two dollars of cash on hand or near-term cash inflows. The extra dollar of current assets provides a margin of safety.

A company could possibly pay its liabilities on time with a current ratio less than 2 to 1, perhaps even if its current ratio were as low as 1 to 1. In this example, the company's three non-interest-bearing liabilities—accounts payable, accrued expenses, and income tax payable—equal 28% of its total current assets. Its banker has lent the business $3,125 thousand on the basis of short-term loans, which is 18% of its total current assets. Its short-term lenders may not be willing to lend the business too much more—although perhaps the business could persuade its banker to go up to, say, $4 or $5 million on short-term notes payable.

In summary, short-term sources of credit generally demand that a company's current assets be double its current liabilities. After all, creditors are not owners—they don't share in the profit earned by the business. The income on their loans is limited to the interest they charge (and collect). As a creditor they quite properly minimize their loan risks; as limited-income (fixed-income) investors they are not compensated to take on much risk.

The Acid Test Ratio (Quick Ratio)

Inventory is many weeks away from conversion into cash. Products are usually held two, three, or four months before being sold. If sales are made on credit, which is normal when one business sells to another business, there's a second waiting period before the receivables are collected. In short, inventory is not nearly as *liquid* as accounts receivable; it takes a lot longer to convert inventory into cash. Furthermore, there's no guarantee that all the products in inventory will be sold.

A more severe measure of the short-term liability-paying ability of a business is the *acid test ratio*, which excludes inventory (and prepaid expenses also). Only cash, marketable securities investments (if any), and accounts receivable are counted as sources to pay the current liabilities of the business.

This ratio is also called the *quick ratio* because only cash and assets quickly convertible into cash are included in the amount available for paying current liabilities. It's more in the nature of a liquidity ratio that focuses on how much cash and near-cash assets a business has to pay all its short-term liabilities.

In this example the company's acid test ratio is calculated as follows (the business has no investments in marketable securities):

$$\frac{\$3,265 \text{ Cash} + \$5,000 \text{ Accounts Receivable}}{\$8,125 \text{ Total Current Liabilities}} = \frac{1.02 \text{ Acid}}{\text{Test Ratio}}$$

The general rule is that a company's acid test ratio should be 1 to 1 or better, although you find many more exceptions to this than with the 2 to 1 current ratio standard.

Debt to Equity Ratio

Some debt is good, but too much is dangerous. The *debt to equity ratio* is an indicator of whether a company is using debt prudently, or perhaps has gone too far and is overburdened with debt that may likely cause problems. For this example the company's debt to equity ratio calculation is:

$$\frac{\$12,375 \text{ Total Liabilities}}{\$23,125 \text{ Total Stockholders' Equity}} = \frac{.54 \text{ Debt to}}{\text{Equity Ratio}}$$

This ratio tells us that the company is using $.54 of liabilities in addition to each $1.00 of stockholders' equity in the business. Notice that *all* liabilities (noninterest as well as interest-bearing, and both short-term and long-term) are included in this ratio, and that *all* owners' equity (invested capital and retained earnings) is included.

This business—with its .54 to 1.00 debt to equity ratio—would be viewed as moderately leveraged. *Leverage* refers to using the equity capital base to raise additional capital from nonowner sources.

In other words, the business is using $1.54 of total capital for every $1.00 of equity capital. So the business has $1.54 of assets working for it for every dollar of equity capital in the business.

Most businesses stay below a 1 to 1 debt to equity ratio. They don't want to take on too much debt, or they cannot convince lenders to put up more than one-half of their assets. However, some capital-intensive (asset-heavy) businesses such as public utilities and most financial institutions operate with debt to equity ratios much higher than 1 to 1.

Times Interest Earned Ratio

To pay interest on its debt a business needs to earn sufficient operating earnings, which is earnings before interest and (income) tax (EBIT). To test the ability to pay interest from earnings, the *times interest earned ratio* is calculated. Annual earnings before interest and income tax is divided by interest expense:

$$\frac{\$4,610 \text{ Operating Earnings}}{\$545 \text{ Interest Expense}} = \begin{array}{c} 8.5 \text{ Times Interest} \\ \text{Earned Ratio} \end{array}$$

There is no standard or general rule for this particular ratio—although obviously the ratio should be higher than 1 to 1. In this example the company's operating earnings are more than 8 times its annual interest expense, which is comforting from the lender's point of view. Lenders would be very alarmed if a business barely covers its annual interest expense. (The company's management should be equally alarmed, of course.)

Profit and Return on Equity Ratios

Making sales while controlling expenses is how a business makes profit. The profit residual "slice" or "cut" from a company's total sales revenue is expressed by the *return on sales ratio*, which is profit divided by sales revenue for the period. The company's return on sales ratio for its latest year is:

$$\frac{\$2,642 \text{ Net Income}}{\$52,000 \text{ Sales Revenue}} = 5.08\% \text{ Return on Sales Ratio}$$

There is another way of explaining the return on sales ratio: For each $100 of sales revenue the business earned $5.08 net income—and had expenses of $94.92. Return on sales varies quite markedly from one industry to another. Some businesses do well with only a 1% or 2% return on sales; others need more than 10% to justify the large amount of capital invested in their assets.

Owners take the risk of whether their business can earn a profit and sustain its profit performance over the years. How much would you pay for a business that consistently suffers a loss? The value of the owners' investment depends first and foremost on the past and future profit performance of the business—or not just profit, I should say, but profit relative to the capital invested to earn that profit.

For instance, suppose a business earns $100,000 annual net income for its stockholders. If its stockholders' equity is only $250,000, then its profit performance relative to the stockholders' capital used to make that profit is 40%, which is very good indeed. If, on the other hand, stockholders' equity is $2,500,000, then the company's profit performance is 4%, which is terrible relative to the owners' capital tied up in the business to earn that profit.

The point is that profit should be compared with the amount of capital invested to earn the profit. Profit for a period divided by the amount of capital invested to earn that profit is called *return on investment* (ROI). ROI is a broad concept that applies to almost any sort of investment of capital.

The owners' investment in a business is the total of the owners' equity accounts in the company's balance sheet. Their profit is bottom-line net income for the period, less dividends that have to be paid on any preferred capital stock shares issued by the business. Preferred stock shares have a first claim on net income. In this example the business has issued only one class of stock shares; the company has no preferred stock, so all of net income belongs to its common stockholders.

Dividing annual net income by stockholders' equity gives the *return on equity* (ROE) ratio. The calculation for the company's ROE in this example is:

$$\frac{\$2,642 \text{ Net Income}}{\$23,125 \text{ Stockholders' Equity*}} = \begin{array}{c} 11.4\% \text{ Return on} \\ \text{Equity Ratio} \end{array}$$

By most standards a 11.4% annual ROE would be acceptable but not impressive. But everything is relative. ROE should be compared with industrywide averages and with investment alternatives. Also, the risk factor is important; just how risky is the stockholders' capital investment in the business?

We would have to know much more about the history and prospects of the business to reach a conclusion regarding whether the 11.4% ROE is good, mediocre, or poor. Also, we would have to consider the opportunity cost of capital—that is, what ROI could be earned by the stockholders on alternative uses for their capital. And we have not considered the income tax factor. Judging ROE is not a simple matter!

Another useful ratio to calculate is the following:

$$\frac{\$4,610 \text{ Operating Earnings}}{\$35,500 \text{ Total Assets*}} = \begin{array}{c} 13.0\% \text{ Return} \\ \text{on Assets Ratio} \end{array}$$

This *return on assets* (ROA) ratio reveals that the business earned $.13 before interest and income tax expenses on each $1.00 assets employed during the year. The ROA is compared with the annual interest rate on the company's borrowed money. In this example the company's annual interest rate on its short-term and long-term debt is 7.5%. The business earned 13.0% on the money borrowed, as measured by the ROA. The difference or spread between the two rates is a favorable 5.5%. This source of profit enhancement is called *financial leverage gain*. If a company's ROA is less than its interest rate it suffers a financial leverage loss.

---

*The ending balance is used to simplify the analysis; alternatively, the weighted average during the year could be used.

Earnings per Share and Price/Earnings Ratios

The capital stock shares of more than 10,000 business corporations are traded in public markets—the New York Stock Exchange, Nasdaq, and other stock exchanges. The day-to-day market price changes of these shares receive a great deal of attention, to say the least! More than any other single factor, the market value of capital stock shares depends on the net income (earnings) performance of a business—its past profit performance and its future profit potential.

Suppose I tell you that the market price of a stock is $60, and ask you whether this value is too high or too low, or just about right. You could compare the market price with the stockholders' equity per share reported in the most recent balance sheet—called the *book value per share*. This is an *asset-based* valuation approach. The company's total assets minus its total liabilities equal its stockholders' equity. The asset-based, or book value method has a respectable history in securities analysis. Today, however, the asset-based approach plays second fiddle to the *earnings-based* approach. The starting point is to calculate earnings (net income) per share.

Earnings per Share (EPS)

One of the most used ratios in stock value and securities analysis is *earnings per share* (EPS). The essential calculation of earnings per share is as follows:

$$\frac{\text{Net Income Available for Common Stockholders}}{\text{Total Number of Outstanding Common Stock Shares*}} = \frac{\text{Basic Earnings}}{\text{per Share}}$$

First, notice that the numerator (top number) in the ratio is *net income available for common stockholders*, which equals bottom-line net income less any dividends paid to the preferred stockholders of the business. Many business corporations issue preferred stock that requires a fixed amount of dividends to be paid each year. The mandatory annual dividends to the preferred stockholders are deducted from net income to determine net income available for the common stockholders. (The preferred stock dividends are *not* reported as an expense; net income is *before* any dividends to stockholders.)

Second, please notice the word *basic* in front of *earnings per share*, which means that the actual number of common stock

---

*To be technically correct, the weighted average number of shares outstanding during the year is used—which takes into account that some shares may have been issued and outstanding only part of the year and that the business may have reduced the number of its outstanding shares during part of the year.

shares in the hands of stockholders is the denominator (bottom number) in the EPS ratio. Many business corporations have entered into contracts of one sort or another that require the company sometime in the future to issue additional stock shares at prices below the market value of its stock shares. But as of yet none of these shares have been actually issued.

For example, business corporations award managers *stock options* to buy common stock shares of the company at fixed prices. If in the future the market value of the shares rises over the fixed option prices the managers can exercise their rights and buy capital stock shares at a bargain price. With stock options, therefore, the number of stock shares is subject to inflation. When (and if) the additional shares are issued, EPS will suffer because net income will have to be spread over a larger number of stock shares. EPS will be diluted, or thinned down, because of the larger denominator in the EPS ratio.*

Basic EPS does *not* recognize the additional shares that would be issued when stock options are exercised. Also, basic EPS does not take into account potential dilution effects of any convertible bonds and convertible preferred stock that have been issued by a business. These securities can be converted at the option of the security holders into common stock shares at predetermined prices.

To warn investors of the potential effects of stock options and convertible securities, a second EPS is reported by public corporations, which is called *diluted EPS*. This lower EPS takes into account the dilution effects caused by the issue of additional common stock shares under stock option plans, convertible securities, and any other commitments a business has entered into that could require it to issue additional stock shares at fixed prices in the future.

Basic EPS and diluted EPS (if applicable) must be reported in

_____

*Accounting for stock options is discussed in Chapter 19, page 140.

the income statements of publicly owned business corporations. This indicates the importance of EPS. In contrast, none of the other ratios discussed in this chapter have to be reported, although many public companies report selected ratios.

Price/Earnings Ratio

The market price of stock shares of a public business corporation is compared with its basic EPS and expressed in the *price/earnings* (P/E) ratio as follows:

$$\frac{\text{Current Market Price of Stock Shares}}{\text{Basic Earnings per Share}} = \frac{\text{Price/Earnings}}{\text{Ratio}}$$

Suppose a company's stock shares are trading at $60 per share and its basic EPS for the most recent year (called the trailing 12 months) is $3. Thus, its P/E ratio is 20. Like other ratios discussed in this chapter, the P/E ratio should be compared with industrywide and marketwide averages to judge whether it's too high or too low. There is no benchmark or standard for what P/E ratios should be. I remember when a P/E ratio of 8 was considered "right." As I write this sentence P/E ratios of 20 or higher are considered acceptable and nothing to be alarmed about.

The P/E ratio is so important that the *Wall Street Journal* and other financial newspapers include it with the trading information for the thousands of stocks traded every business day on the national stock exchanges.

There are no market prices for the stock shares of a privately owned or nonpublic business because the shares are not traded, or when they are sold the price is not made public. Nevertheless, stockholders in these businesses want to know what their shares are worth. To estimate the value of stock shares a P/E multiple can be used. In the company example, basic EPS is $3.30 for the most recent year (see Exhibit 22.1, page 170). Suppose you own some of the capital stock shares, and someone offers to buy your shares. You could establish an offer price at, say, 12 times basic EPS. This gives about $40 per share. The potential buyer may not be willing to pay this price, or he or she might be willing to pay 15 or 18 times basic EPS.

Earnings Yield and Market Cap

The reciprocal or flip-flop of the P/E ratio is the E/P ratio, which is called the *earnings yield*. Imagine for the moment that the company in our example is a publicly owned business. Its basic EPS is $3.30.

Suppose its capital stock is trading at $65 per share. Thus, its earnings yield would be:

$$\frac{\$3.30 \text{ Basic EPS}}{\$65 \text{ Market Price}} = 5.1\% \text{ Earnings Yield}$$

This means that the company is earning annual net income equal to 5.1% of the current market price of the stock shares.

The *market cap*, or total market value capitalization of the company, is $52,026 thousand ($65 market value per share × 800,400 capital stock shares = $52,026 thousand). This is more than owners' equity reported in the company's balance sheet, which is only $23,125 thousand. Market caps are much higher than the book values of owners' equity reported in balance sheets of most companies.

Final Comments

Many other ratios can be calculated from the data in financial statements. For example, the *asset turnover ratio* (annual sales revenue divided by total assets) and the *dividend yield* (annual cash dividends per share divided by market value per share) are two ratios you often see used in securities analysis. There's no end to the ratios that can be calculated.

The trick is to focus on those ratios that have the most interpretive value. Of course it's not easy to figure out which ratios are the most important. Professional investors tend to use too many ratios rather than too few, in my opinion. But, you never know which ratio might provide a valuable clue to the future market value increase or decrease of a stock.

23

A LOOK INSIDE MANAGEMENT ACCOUNTING

Unless you happened to start reading the book in this chapter you know that the previous chapters deal with the *external financial statements* reported by businesses. Accounting involves more than preparing a company's external financial statements, although this is certainly one of the most important functions.

Every business must install an *accounting system*, including forms, procedures, records, reports, computer hardware and software, and personnel, to keep the day-to-day activities of a business running smoothly and to prevent delays and stoppages. Internal accounting controls should be enforced to deter and detect errors and fraud.

Many *tax returns* have to be filed by every business—for income taxes, property taxes, sales taxes, and payroll taxes. Accountants are in charge of tax compliance.

Accounting systems, tax accounting, and financial accounting (preparing external financial statements) are three bedrock functions. Accounting has another primary function—to provide information needed by managers for their decision making, planning, and control. This fourth fundamental function of accounting is called *management accounting* or managerial accounting.

A brief excursion into this branch of accounting is very helpful for understanding the limits of external financial statements and appreciating the differences between *external* financial reports to investors and lenders and *internal* accounting reports to managers of a business. This chapter is like a gate in the wall between external and internal accounting that you can walk through to have a look around the other side.

This chapter introduces the topic of management accounting. To be frank, the chapter is no more than a skimpy appetizer compared with the full-course menu of management accounting. For a fuller treatment of the topic I can recommend my book *The Fast Forward MBA in Finance*, Second Edition (John Wiley & Sons, 2002).

First Things about Management Accounting

Management accounting is an *internal* function that operates within the boundaries of a business to help managers make sound decisions, develop plans and goals, and exercise control. The basic purpose of management accounting is to help managers be better managers. Management accounting, more than anything else, involves providing useful information to managers and helping them use this information in the most effective manner.

The design of accounting reports for managers is very dependent on the nature of the business and how the business is organized. If a business is divided into several sales territories, for example, accounting reports are organized by sales territories. Within each sales territory the business may be organized by major product lines. So, the accounting reports separate out each product line in each territory.

In short, management accounting follows the organizational structure of a business. This chapter focuses on the profit report to top-level managers of a business who have companywide responsibility. The chapter looks at the top of the organizational pyramid, and takes a summit point of view of the business.

The external financial statements of a business are not completely adequate for its top-level managers, despite the fact that these financials are for the company as a whole. This is not a knock on external financial statements, which are designed for the outside investors and lenders of the business and not for its managers. Managers should understand their company's external financial statements like the backs of their hands. But they need additional accounting reports that are much more detailed.

In particular, the external income statement is not a good explanation of *profit behavior*—especially for management analysis. All managers who have profit responsibility need a hands-on model that provides a clear pathway to profit. The next section introduces a management profit model. The profit model should make transparent the basic factors and variables that drive profit and how they all fit together to arrive at bottom-line profit (net income). A profit model should serve as a blueprint for constructing, maintaining, and improving the bottom line of the business.

One Word of Caution: Management accounting is an art, not a science. There are no authoritative standards, and no generally accepted management accounting principles that govern management accounting. Tax accounting must follow tax laws and regulations and use prescribed tax forms. External financial statements have to be prepared in accordance with generally accepted accounting principles (GAAP). Management accounting is a wide-open game with few ground rules.

Management Accounting Centerpiece:
The Profit Model

Suppose you have just hired on as the new president and CEO of a business. Your compensation package includes a bonus that depends on improving the profit performance of the business. This business is smaller than the company example used throughout earlier chapters. You've studied the internal profit reports used by the business in the past, and you don't like them. So, you've engaged me to recommend a profit report that would be better for your decision-making, planning, and control purposes.

I present to you the profit report shown in Exhibit 23.1 on page 186. It contains highly confidential information that would not be released outside the business. Exhibit 23.1 presents an inside look at how the business made the $718,200 profit (bottom-line net income) for the year just ended, and includes a comparison with the previous year. The business did better than last period. The profit report provides the information to analyze the reasons for the profit improvement.

Let me say immediately that the design of this illustrative management profit report reflects my personal preferences. There are no standard formats or templates for these types of accounting reports. This exhibit is not necessarily the ideal format for all businesses in every respect.

The purpose of Exhibit 23.1 is to demonstrate several critical points. I do not mean to suggest that the exhibit is a universal format that does not need to be changed from company to company. On the other hand, Exhibit 23.1 serves as a road map that a business could adapt to its particular needs.

As just mentioned, the profit report is designed for the president of the business, who has broad responsibility. The corporation's board of directors can also use this report for their year-end review of the profit performance of the business. The exhibit is not designed for a manager with limited authority and responsibility, such as the sales manager or production department supervisor.

The profit model shown in Exhibit 23.1 has a twofold purpose: (1) to show what information is needed for management analysis of profit behavior that focuses on the key variables that drive profit; and (2) to highlight "control points," which are the critical factors that have high impact on profit performance.

Notice under each line in the management profit report shown in Exhibit 23.1 that there are bullets for one or more control points. For example, the number of employees and the annual sales per employee are shown under the net sales revenue line. Under the total fixed operating expenses line are two important costs—advertising and other marketing expenses, and senior management compensation. The president should keep an eye on these two expenditures.

In the limited space of this chapter I can offer only a brief overview of how business managers use a profit report. Speaking broadly, most analysis focuses on *changes*. Every factor and variable that determines profit is subject to change; change is constant, as any experienced business manager will verify.

Business managers need a profit model that they actually can work with, one that they can make changes to like pulling handles on a machine—to quickly measure the impact of the changes on profit.

Managers must respond to changes in the profit factors in order to maintain the profit performance of the business. For example, higher transportation costs next year may increase the sales volume driven expenses from $4.50 per unit sold (see Exhibit 23.1) to $4.85. Or, property taxes may go up, which will increase fixed operating expenses. Or, the sales manager may make a persuasive case that the advertising budget should be increased next year. Managers have to respond to all such changes; they don't get paid to sit on their hands and idly watch the changes happen.

Top-level managers have the responsibility of developing realistic plans to improve profit performance, which means making changes in the profit equation of the business. Which specific changes? This is the key question. Suppose the president asked you to develop a plan to improve bottom-line net income 10% next year. Exactly how would you accomplish this goal? I'd suggest that you should construct your plan in terms of the specific factors and variables in the profit model that you will change to bring off the 10% profit improvement.

To illustrate the use of a profit model such as the one shown in Exhibit 23.1, let me put a question to you. Assume that all the factors and variables in the profit model remain the same next year—except that sales price or sales volume will change next year, but not both. Which alternative is better for profit?

+ Increase sales price 5% next year.
+ Increase sales volume 10% next year.

Of course it would be best to make both changes (without any unfavorable changes in the other factors). But I'm putting it to you as an either-or choice. You could do only one or the other. Which alternative would increase bottom-line profit more?

I have entered the profit model shown in Exhibit 23.1 in an Excel work sheet. So, I simply changed sales price +5% for one alternative, and changed sales volume +10% for the other alternative. The outputs for the two scenarios are shown in Exhibits 23.2 and 23.3 on the following pages.

Before looking at the results, you might ask yourself which alternative you think is better. I suspect that many persons would select the second alternative because the sales volume increase is much more than the sales price increase. However, the model shows that the sales price increase alternative is quite a bit better.

The sales manager of the company might push for the sales volume alternative because the business would increase its market share at the higher sales volume. Market share is always an important factor to consider—I wouldn't ignore this point. But, if you compare the two alternatives, bumping the sales price 5% would be much better for profit.

The main reason why the sales price alternative is so much better is that the *contribution profit margin* increases 20% in this scenario. Because of the sales price increase, the margin increases $4.78 per unit ($28.36 at the higher sales price minus $23.58 at the old sales price = $4.78 increase per unit, or 20% higher). The sales price hike pushes up total contribution margin 20%, which is a substantial gain in profit before fixed operating expenses, interest, and income tax. Bottom-line profit would increase from $718,200 to $1,005,240 (see Exhibit 23.2).

In contrast, the sales volume increase scenario improves total contribution margin just 10%, which is equal to the sales volume increase (see Exhibit 23.3). Of course, it may be more realistic to sell 10% more sales volume compared with pushing through a 5%

EXHIBIT 23.1—ILLUSTRATION OF AN INTERNAL CONFIDENTIAL PROFIT REPORT TO TOP-LEVEL MANAGERS

	Most Recent Period			Comparable Previous Period		
Sales Volume (Total Units Sold)	100,000 units			85,800 units		
	Per Unit	**Totals**	**Control Points**	**Per Unit**	**Totals**	**Control Points**
Net Sales Revenue	$104.00	$10,400,000		$100.00	$8,580,000	
• Sales per Employee (Head Count: 77 and 67)			$135,065			$128,060
Cost of Goods Sold	(67.60)	(6,760,000)		(68.75)	(5,898,750)	
• Inventory Shrinkage and Write-Downs			($126,700)			($293,400)
Gross Margin, before Operating Expenses	$ 36.40	$ 3,640,000		$ 31.25	$2,681,250	
• Return on Sales			35.0%			31.5%
Variable Operating Expenses						
• Sales Volume Driven Expenses	(4.50)	(450,000)		(4.10)	(351,780)	
• Sales Revenue Driven Expenses	(8.32)	(832,000)	−8.00%	(7.50)	(643,500)	−7.50%
Contribution Profit Margin	$ 23.58	$ 2,358,000		$ 19.65	$1,685,970	
• Return on Sales			22.7%			19.7%
Total Fixed Operating Expenses		(1,058,000)			(862,500)	
• Advertising and Other Marketing Expenses			($226,000)			($146,000)
• Senior Management Compensation			($628,000)			($549,000)
Operating Profit		$ 1,300,000			$ 823,470	
• Return on Sales			12.5%			9.6%
Interest Expense		(103,000)			(96,000)	
• Average Annual Interest Rate on Debt			8.00%			8.0%
Earnings before Income Tax		$ 1,197,000			$ 727,470	
Income Tax Expense		(478,800)			(290,988)	
• Effective Tax Rate			40.0%			40.0%
Net Income		$ 718,200			$ 436,482	
• Return on Sales			6.9%			5.1%

EXHIBIT 23.2—SCENARIO FOR +5% SALES PRICE INCREASE

	Most Recent Period			+5% Sales Price Next Period		
Sales Volume (Total Units Sold)	100,000 units			100,000 units		
	Per Unit	**Totals**	**Control Points**	**Per Unit**	**Totals**	**Control Points**
Net Sales Revenue	$104.00	$10,400,000		$109.20	$10,920,000	
• Sales per Employee (Head Count: 77 and 67)			$135,065			$141,818
Cost of Goods Sold	(67.60)	(6,760,000)		(67.60)	(6,760,000)	
• Inventory Shrinkage and Write-Downs			($126,700)			($126,700)
Gross Margin, before Operating Expenses	$ 36.40	$ 3,640,000		$ 41.60	$ 4,160,000	
• Return on Sales			35.0%			38.1%
Variable Operating Expenses						
• Sales Volume Driven Expenses	(4.50)	(450,000)		(4.50)	(450,000)	
• Sales Revenue Driven Expenses	(8.32)	(832,000)	−8.00%	(8.74)	(873,600)	−8.00%
Contribution Profit Margin	$ 23.58	$ 2,358,000		$ 28.36	$ 2,836,400	
• Return on Sales			22.7%			26.0%
Total Fixed Operating Expenses		(1,058,000)			(1,058,000)	
• Advertising and Other Marketing Expenses			($226,000)			($226,000)
• Senior Management Compensation			($628,000)			($628,000)
Operating Profit		$ 1,300,000			$ 1,778,400	
• Return on Sales			12.5%			16.3%
Interest Expense		(103,000)			(103,000)	
• Average Annual Interest Rate on Debt			8.00%			8.0%
Earnings before Income Tax		$ 1,197,000			$ 1,675,400	
Income Tax Expense		(478,800)			(670,160)	
• Effective Tax Rate			40.0%			40.0%
Net Income		$ 718,200			$ 1,005,240	
• Return on Sales			6.9%			9.2%

EXHIBIT 23.3—SCENARIO FOR +10% SALES VOLUME INCREASE

	MOST RECENT PERIOD			+10% SALES VOLUME NEXT PERIOD		
Sales Volume (Total Units Sold)	100,000 units			110,000 units		
	Per Unit	**Totals**	**Control Points**	**Per Unit**	**Totals**	**Control Points**
Net Sales Revenue	$104.00	$10,400,000		$104.00	$11,440,000	
• Sales per Employee (Head Count: 77 and 67)			$ 135,065			$148,571
Cost of Goods Sold	(67.60)	(6,760,000)		(67.60)	(7,436,000)	
• Inventory Shrinkage and Write-Downs			($126,700)			($126,700)
Gross Margin, before Operating Expenses	$ 36.40	$ 3,640,000		$ 36.40	$ 4,004,000	
• Return on Sales			35.0%			35.0%
Variable Operating Expenses						
• Sales Volume Driven Expenses	(4.50)	(450,000)		(4.50)	(495,000)	
• Sales Revenue Driven Expenses	(8.32)	(832,000)	−8.00%	(8.32)	(915,200)	−8.00%
Contribution Profit Margin	$ 23.58	$ 2,358,000		$ 23.58	$ 2,593,800	
• Return on Sales			22.7%			22.7%
Total Fixed Operating Expenses		(1,058,000)			(1,058,000)	
• Advertising and Other Marketing Expenses			($226,000)			($226,000)
• Senior Management Compensation			($628,000)			($628,000)
Operating Profit		$ 1,300,000			$ 1,535,800	
• Return on Sales			12.5%			13.4%
Interest Expense		(103,000)			(103,000)	
• Average Annual Interest Rate on Debt			8.00%			8.0%
Earnings before Income Tax		$ 1,197,000			$ 1,432,800	
Income Tax Expense		(478,800)			(573,120)	
• Effective Tax Rate			40.0%			40.0%
Net Income		$ 718,200			$ 859,680	
• Return on Sales			6.9%			7.5%

sales price increase. Many customers may balk at the higher sales price and take their business elsewhere.

Setting sales prices certainly is one of the most perplexing decisions facing business managers. The price sensitivity of customers is never clear-cut. In any case, business managers should understand that a relatively small change in sales price can have a major impact on profit margin. For instance, a 10% shift in sales price can cause a twofold, threefold, or even higher impact on profit margin.

24

A FEW PARTING COMMENTS

Some years ago a local women's investment club invited me to their monthly meeting to talk about the meaning and uses of financial reports. It was a lot of fun, and it also forced me to rethink a few basic points. These women are a sophisticated group of investors who pool their monthly contributions and invest mainly in common stocks traded on the New York Stock Exchange. Several of their questions were incisive, although one point caught me quite by surprise.

As I recall at that time they were thinking of buying 100 common stock shares in General Electric (GE). Two members presented their research on the company with the recommendation to buy the stock at the going market price. The discussion caused me to suspect that several of the members thought their money would go to GE. I pointed out that no, the money would go to the seller of the stock shares, not to GE.

They were not clear on the fundamental difference between the *primary capital market* (the original issue of securities by corporations for money that flows directly into their coffers), which is entirely separate from the *secondary capital market* (in which people sell securities they already own to other investors, with no money going to the corporations that originally issued the securities). I compared this with the purchase of a new car in which money goes to GM, Ford, or Chrysler (through the dealer) versus the purchase of a used car in which the money goes to the previous owner.

We cleared up that point, although I think they were disappointed that GE would not get their money. Once I pointed out the distinction between the two capital markets they realized that while they were of the opinion that the going market value was a good price to buy at, the person on the other side of the trade must think it was a good price to *sell* at.

On other matters they asked very thoughtful questions. I'd like to share these with you in this chapter, as well as a few other points that are important for anyone investing in stock and debt securities issued by corporations. These questions are also important when buying a business *as a whole*—for corporate raiders attempting hostile takeovers; corporate managers engineering a leveraged buyout of the business; one corporation taking over another; or an individual purchasing a closely held business. Buyouts and takeovers bring up the business valuation question, which is discussed briefly.

Some Basic Questions and Answers

Investors in corporate stock and debt securities should know the answers to the following fundamental questions concerning financial statements. These questions are answered from the viewpoint of the typical individual investor, *not* an institutional investor or professional investment manager. My retirement fund manages over $200 billion of investments. I assume its portfolio managers already know the answers to these questions. They'd better!

♦ **Are financial statements reliable and trustworthy?**

Yes, the vast majority of audited financial statements are presented fairly according to established standards, which are called generally accepted accounting principles. If not, the CPA auditor calls deviations or shortcomings to your attention. So, be sure to read the auditor's report. You should realize, however, that financial accounting standards are not static. Over time these profit measurement methods and disclosure practices change and evolve.

Accounting's rule-making authorities constantly monitor financial reporting practices and problem areas. They make changes when needed, especially to keep abreast of changes in business and financial practices, as well as developments in the broader political, legal, and economic world that business operates in. (See Chapter 19 for review.)

♦ **Nevertheless, are some financial statements misleading and fraudulent?**

Yes, unfortunately. The *Wall Street Journal* and the *New York Times*, for example, carry many stories of high-level management fraud—illegal payments, misuse of assets, and known losses were concealed; expenses were underrecorded; sales revenues were overrecorded or sales returns were not recorded; off-balance sheet entities were used to hide debt of the business; and financial distress symptoms were buried out of sight.

It is very difficult for CPA auditors to detect high-level management fraud that has been cleverly concealed or that involves a conspiracy among managers and other parties to the fraud. (See Chapter 17 for review of audits by CPAs.) Auditors are highly skilled professionals, and the rate of audit failures has been low. Sometimes, however, the auditors were lax in their duties and deserved to be sued—and were! CPA firms have paid hundreds and hundreds of millions of dollars to defrauded investors and creditors.

There's always a small risk that the financial statements are, in fact, false or misleading. You would have legal recourse against the company's managers and its auditors once the fraud is found out, but this is not a happy situation. Almost certainly you'd still end up losing money, even after recovering some of your losses though legal action.

◆ Is it worth your time as an individual investor to read carefully through the financial statements and also to compute ratios and make other interpretations?

I doubt it. The women's investment club was very surprised by this answer, and I don't blame them. The conventional wisdom is that by diligent reading of financial statements you will discover under- or overvalued securities. But the evidence doesn't support this premise. Market prices reflect all publicly available information about a business, including the information in its latest quarterly and annual financial reports.

If you enjoy reading through financial statements, as I do, fine. It's a valuable learning experience. But don't expect to find out something that the market doesn't already know. It's very unlikely that you will find a nugget of information that has been overlooked by everyone else. Forget it; it's not worth your time as an investor. The same time would be better spent keeping up with current developments reported in the financial press.

◆ Why should you read financial statements, then?

To know what you are getting into. Does the company have a lot of debt and a heavy interest load to carry? For that matter, is the company in bankruptcy or in a debt workout situation? Has the company had a consistent earnings record over the past 5 to 10 years, or has its profit ridden a roller coaster over this time? Has the company consistently paid cash dividends for many years? Has the company issued more than one class of stock? Which stock are you buying, relative to any other classes?

You would obviously inspect a house before getting serious about buying it, to see if it has two stories, three or more bedrooms, a basement, a good general appearance, and so on. Likewise, you should know the "financial architecture" of a business before putting your capital in its securities. Financial statements serve this getting-acquainted purpose very well.

One basic stock investment strategy is to search through financial reports, or financial statement data stored in computer databases, to find corporations that meet certain criteria—for example, whose market values are less than their book values, whose cash and cash equivalent per share are more than a certain percent of their current market value, and so on. Whether these stocks end up beating the market is another matter. In any case, financial statements can be culled to find whatever types of corporations you are looking for.

◆ Is there any one basic "litmus test" for a quick test on a company's financial performance?

Yes. I would suggest that you compute the percent increase (or decrease) in sales revenue this year compared with last year, and use this percent as the baseline for testing changes in bottom-line profit (net income) as well as the major operating assets of the business. Assume sales revenue increased 10% over last year. Did profit increase 10%? Did accounts receivable, inventory, and long-term operating assets increase 10%?

This is no more than a quick-and-dirty method, but it will point out major disparities. For instance, suppose inventory jumped 50% even though sales revenue increased only 10%. This may signal a major management mistake; the overstock of inventory might lead to write-downs later. Management does not usually comment on such disparities in financial reports. You'll have to find them yourself.

◆ Do conservative accounting methods cause conservative market values?

For publicly owned corporations that have active trading in their securities, the general answer would seem to be no. Many businesses select conservative accounting methods to measure profit, which results in conservative book values for their assets and liabilities. On occasion even conservative methods can cause opposite effects (i.e., higher earnings) in a particular year because of such things as LIFO liquidation gains in that year. (See Chapter 20 for review.)

The evidence suggests that securities markets take into account differences in profit measurement methods between companies in determining stock market values. In other words, the market is not fooled by differences in accounting methods, even though earnings, assets, and liabilities are reported by different methods of accounting from company to company.

To be honest, this is not an easy general conclusion to prove. There are exceptions, but not on any consistent basis. Overall, differences in accounting methods seem to be adjusted for in the marketplace. For instance, a business could not simply switch its accounting methods to improve the market value of its stock shares. The market will not react this way; investors do not blindly follow accounting numbers.

I advise caution and careful attention to accounting methods when you are considering buying or making a major investment in a *privately held* business for which there is no market to establish values for the stock shares issued by the business.

◆ Do financial statements report the truth, the whole truth, and nothing but the truth?

There are really two separate questions here. One question concerns how truthful is profit accounting, which depends on a company's choice of accounting methods from the menu of generally accepted alternatives and how faithfully the methods are applied year in and year out. The other question concerns how honest and forthright is the disclosure in a company's financial report.

Profit should be faithful to the accounting methods adopted by the business. In other words, once accounting choices have been made, the business should apply the methods and let the chips fall where they may. However, there is convincing evidence that managers occasionally, if not regularly, intervene in the application of their profit accounting methods to produce more favorable results than would otherwise happen—something akin to the "thumb on the scale" approach.

This is done to smooth reported earnings, to balance out unwanted perturbations and oscillations in annual earnings. Investors seem to prefer a nice steady trend of earnings instead of fluctuations, and managers oblige. So, be warned that annual earnings probably are smoothed to some extent. (See Chapter 18 for review.)

Disclosure in financial reports is quite another matter. The majority of companies are reluctant to lay bare all the facts. Bad news is usually suppressed or at least deemphasized as long as possible. Clearly, there is a lack of candor and frank discussion in many financial reports. Few companies are willing to wash their dirty linen in public by making full disclosure of their mistakes and difficulties in their financial reports.

There is a management discussion and analysis (MD&A) section in financial reports. But usually this is a fairly sanitized version of what happened during the year. The history of financial reporting disclosure practices, unfortunately, makes clear that until standard-setting authorities force specific disclosure standards on all companies, few make such disclosures voluntarily.

Some years ago the disclosure of employee pension and retirement costs went through this pattern of inadequate reporting until, finally, the standard-setting bodies stepped in and required fuller disclosure. Until a standard was issued, few companies reported a cash flow statement, even though this statement had been asked for by security analysts since the 1950s! Recalls of unsafe products, pending lawsuits, and top management compensation are other examples of "reluctant reporting."

The masthead of the *New York Times* boasts "All the News That's Fit to Print." Don't expect this in companies' financial reports, however.

◆ Does a financial report explain the basic profit-making strategy of the business?

Not really. In an ideal world, I would argue, a financial report should not merely report how much profit (net income) was earned by the business and the amounts of revenue and expenses that generated this profit. The financial report should also provide a profit road map, or an earnings blueprint of the business. Financial report readers should be told the basic profit-making strategy of the business, including its most critical profit-making success factors.

In their annual financial reports publicly owned corporations are required to disclose their sales revenue and operating expenses by major segments (lines of business); this provides information about which product lines are more profitable than others. However, segments are very large, conglomerate totals that span many different products. Segment disclosure was certainly a step in the right direction. For example, the breakdown between domestic versus international sales revenue and operating profit is very important for many businesses.

Businesses do not report the profit margins of their key product lines. Both security analysts and professional investment managers focus much attention on profit margins, but you don't find this information in financial reports. And you don't find any separation between fixed as opposed to variable expenses in external income statements, which is essential for meaningful profit analysis.

In management accounting, you quickly learn that the first step is to go back to square one and recast the income statement into a management planning and decision making structure that focuses on profit margins and cost behavior. (See Exhibit 23.1 on page 186 for an example.)

In short, the income statement you find in an external financial report is not what you would see if you were the CEO of the business. Profit information is considered very confidential, to be kept away not only from competitors but from the investors in the business as well.

◆ Do financial statements report the value of the business as a whole?

No. The balance sheet of a business does not report what the market value of a company would be on the auction block. Financial statements are prepared on the *going concern, historical cost* accounting basis—not on a *current market value* basis. Until there is a serious buyer or an actual takeover attempt it's anyone's guess how much a business would fetch. A buyer may be willing to pay much more than or only a fraction of the owners' equity (book value) reported in its most recent balance sheet.

The market value of a publicly owned corporation's stock shares is not tied to the book value of its stock shares. (See Chapter 22 for review.) Market value, whether you are talking about a business as a whole or per share of a publicly owned corporation, is a negotiated price between a buyer and seller and depends on factors other than book value.

Generally speaking, there is no reason to estimate current replacement cost values for a company's assets and current settlement values of its liabilities.* Furthermore, even it this were done these values do not determine the market value of stock shares or the business as a whole.

The market value of a business as a whole or its stock shares depends mainly on its profit-making ability projected into the future. A buyer may be willing to pay 20 times or more the annual net income of a closely owned, privately held business or 20 times or more the latest earnings per share of publicly owned corporations. Investors keep a close watch on the price/earnings (P/E) ratios of stock shares issued by publicly owned corporations. (See Chapter 22 for review.)

Also, it should be mentioned that earnings-based values are quite different from liquidation-based values for a business. Suppose a company is in bankruptcy proceedings or in a troubled debt workout situation. In this unhappy position the claims of its debt securities and other liabilities dominate the value of its stock shares and owners' equity. Indeed, the stock shares may have no value in such cases.

◆ Should financial statements be taken at face value when buying a business?

No. The potential buyer of a business as a whole (or the controlling interest in a business) should have in hand the latest financial statements of the company. The financial statements are the essential point of reference but are just a good point of departure for many questions. For example, are book values good indicators of the current market and replacement values of the company's assets?

Current values usually are close to book values for some assets—marketable securities, accounts receivable, and FIFO-based inventory. On the other hand, book values of LIFO-based inventory, long-term operating assets depreciated by accelerated methods, and land purchased many years ago may be far below current market and replacement values.

Cash is usually a hard number, although a buyer should be aware that there may be some *window dressing*.† Every asset other than cash presents potential valuation problems. For example, a business may not have written off all of its uncollectible accounts receivable. Some of its inventory may be unsalable, but not yet written down. Some of its fixed assets may be obsolete and in fact may have been placed in the mothball fleet, yet these assets may still be on the books.

Some potential or contingent liabilities may not be recorded, such as lawsuits in progress. In short, a buyer probably will have to do some housecleaning on the assets and liabilities of the business, and then start negotiations on the basis of these adjusted amounts.

A potential buyer should also ask to see the internal management profit reports of the business, but management may be reluctant to provide this confidential information. For that

---

*Exceptions to this general rule are when a value has to be put on the stock shares of a privately owned business for estate tax purposes or in a divorce settlement.

---

†Window dressing refers to holding the books open a few days after the close of the year to record cash receipts as if the money had been received by the end of the year, to build up the cash balance reported in the ending balance sheet. Unfortunately, this practice is tolerated by CPA auditors.

matter, the business may not have a very good management reporting system. The buyer can ask for information about product costs and sales prices to get a rough idea of profit margins. In short, the buyer needs both the external income statements of the business and its internal management information as well.

A business might have certain valuable assets that the buyer wants for the purpose of selling them off, or the buyer may be planning radical changes in the financial structure of the business. There have been cases of a buyer paying less than a company's net cash amount—cash and cash equivalents minus liabilities. In other words, the buyer bought in for less than the immediate liquidation value of the business. This is very rare, of course.

A Short Summary

I remain confident that you can rely on audited financial statements, although the rash of accounting frauds during recent years that CPA auditors failed to discover certainly shook my confidence somewhat. Overall, the percent of fraudulent financial reports among all public businesses is still very low. In any case, investors don't really have an alternative source of financial information about a business other than its financial statements. Accounting fraud, unfortunately, is an unavoidable risk of investing.

You might think twice before investing much time in analyzing the financial statements of corporations whose securities are publicly traded—because hundreds of other investors have done the same analysis and the chance of you finding out something that no one else has yet discovered is nil. For a quick benchmark test, though, you might compare the percent change in the company's sale revenue over last year with the percent changes in its net income and operating assets. Major disparities are worth a look.

Reading financial statements is the best way of getting acquainted with the financial structure of a business that you're thinking of investing in. Don't worry too much about businesses that use conservative accounting methods. There seems to be no adverse effect on the market value of their stock shares. For privately owned companies, on the other hand, you should keep an eye on the major accounting policies of the business and how these accounting methods affect reported earnings and asset values.

Disclosure in financial statements leaves a lot to be desired. Don't look for a road map of the profit strategy of a business in its financial reports. Keep in mind that the total value of a business is not to be found in its balance sheet. Until an actual buyer of a business makes a serious offer there is no particular reason to determine the value of the business as a going concern. Value depends mainly on the past earnings record of the business as forecast into the future.

The main message of this final chapter is to be prudent and careful in making decisions based on financial statements. Many investors and managers don't seem to be fully aware of the limitations of financial statements. Used intelligently, financial reports are the indispensable starting point for investment and lending decisions. I hope my book helps you make better decisions. Good luck, and be careful out there.

INDEX